TABLE OF CONTENTS

Preface v
1. Public Profession of Faith 1
2. The Origins of Profession of Faith 6
3. Profession of Faith in the Ancient Church 11
4. Profession of Faith in the Reformation 18
5. Profession of Faith and Baptism 30
6. Profession of Faith and the Doctrines of Scripture ... 37
7. The Relationship Between Profession of Faith and Faith .. 47
8. Profession of Faith Before God and His Church 62
9. Profession of Faith and the Lord's Supper 72
10. Profession of Faith and the Church 95
11. Profession of Faith and the World 105
12. Profession of Faith and the Good Fight of Faith 122

CALLED TO CONFESS

CORNELIS HARINCK

Translated by Bartel Elshout

REFORMATION HERITAGE BOOKS
Grand Rapids, Michigan

Copyright © 2003
Reformation Heritage Books
2919 Leonard St., NE, Grand Rapids, Michigan 49525
Phone: 616-977-0599 / Fax: 616-285-3246
e-mail: orders@heritagebooks.org
website: www.heritagebooks.org

ISBN # 1-892777-28-2

All rights reserved. Printed in the United States of America.

This book is a translation of *Tot belijden geroepen*
(Leiden: J.J. Groen en Zoon, 1994).
We are grateful to the publishers for permission to print this title in English.

*For additional Reformed literature, request a
free book list from the above addresses.*

Preface

It is a moment of profound importance when young people, after having been faithfully catechized by the church, publicly confess that they believe Jesus is the Christ, the Savior of sinners, and that they want to put their trust in Him alone for salvation.

When profession of faith is made before the congregation, we witness the visible confirmation of God's covenant faithfulness, for God promises in His Word that He will build His church from generation to generation. Public profession of faith is therefore intimately connected with, and an outgrowth of, the baptism of these young people. When they were baptized as infants, they received the mark of God's covenant, confirming their membership in the visible church of Jesus Christ. At that time, their parents publicly reaffirmed their profession of faith and made a solemn vow that, to the utmost of their ability, they would raise their children in harmony with this profession.

Public profession of faith marks the moment when young people assume full responsibility for this profession, promising to maintain it and to adorn it with a godly life. At the same time, this profession allows them to partake of the sacraments; that is, they may partake of the Lord's Supper, and in due time may present their own children for baptism.

Thus, not only is there an intimate connection between baptism and public profession of faith but also between public profession of faith and partaking of the Lord's Supper. Reformed and Presbyterian orthodox churches have some difference of opinion regarding the latter connection. Some churches insist that all who publicly profess faith are obligated to partake of the Lord's Supper to affirm that they believe in the Lord Jesus Christ. Failure to do so might result in the exercise of Christian discipline. Other churches so stress the need for self-examination and possessing various marks of grace that few people who profess their faith publicly take the opportunity to partake of the Lord's Supper. In those churches, the connection between public profession of faith and the Lord's Supper is so minimized that profession of faith is reduced to a mere confession of the doctrinal truths of the Christian religion. It is thus quite possible to be a full member in good standing while never partaking of the Lord's Supper.

How should we address this issue? How can we preserve the important link between public profession of faith and the Lord's Supper without encouraging presumptuous attendance at the Lord's Table? How can we guard against reducing public profession of faith to a mere confession of truth? How can we maintain the proper relationship between baptism and a baptized person's responsibility to profess faith in Christ and show forth His death in the midst of the congregation? How can we encourage every confessing member to engage in thorough self-examination before coming to the Lord's Table?

Those looking for answers to these questions would do well to read this book. The author deals with these issues thoroughly and with the maturity born of forty years of pastoral ministry.

Cornelis Harinck begins by examining the practices of the early Christian church. He shows that many of our current practices regarding profession of faith are rooted in the ancient church. He then moves to the Reformation and from it draws truths that apply to our present setting. His interaction with the biblical, confessional, and historical data regarding this subject is most profitable.

Since every generation grapples with these issues, we recommend that pastors and office-bearers carefully study this book. It will greatly help them guide young people as they approach the years of discretion when they should seriously consider public profession of faith. Church consistories, councils, or sessions might want to give a copy of this book to each young person who attends classes in preparation for making public profession of faith. Teachers could also offer reading assignments in this book as the class progresses. Young people who have already made profession of faith would also benefit from reading this book.

We pray that the Lord may richly bless the reading of this book so that the practice of making public profession of faith will function in a biblically balanced way in Reformed and Presbyterian churches. May this book help young people take the matter of making public profession of faith seriously and guide them to understand their responsibilities and privileges. Above all, may they be led by the Holy Spirit to the great object of saving faith, our blessed Lord Jesus Christ.

—Joel R. Beeke and Bartel Elshout

Author's Preface

Dear young friend,

I have decided to write a book about making profession of faith, since you will not find much literature that addresses questions you might have regarding this matter. By having researched the historical roots of making profession of faith, I believe I have shed considerable light upon the views of the more recent church regarding profession of faith by baptized young people. We too easily forget that there is a link between the church today and the biblical and historical tradition of the Christian church.

I have sought to answer the heart's questions of all who desire to make profession of faith, even though the true answer is to be found with God alone.

I have also attempted to be as comprehensive as possible in my approach; hence the various chapters about the church, doctrine, and the world. This book has not been written merely for those young people who either are making profession of faith or have already done so. Read this book prior to making profession of faith.

On the one hand, I hope that after reading this book you will no longer be able to make profession of faith thoughtlessly. On the other hand, however, I hope that after reading it you will be convicted that you cannot avoid making profession of faith.

— Rev. C. Harinck

Houten, the Netherlands, January 1994

—1—
PUBLIC PROFESSION OF FAITH

Are you a Spectator or Are You Running in the Race?
What is the goal of those who run in a race? To obtain the prize, of course! Every participant wants to finish first and to acquire the gold medal. In Greece, the spectators would shout to the participants during the race: "*Brabeion, brabeion!*" Our word "bravo" is derived from this. It means as much as: "The prize, the prize! Think of the prize after the victory!"

This is also true when running the race of faith, for in this race there is also a prize to be obtained: the prize of eternal life. Paul writes, "So run, that ye may obtain" (1 Cor. 9:24). In this race you cannot merely run leisurely, but you must run to obtain the prize.

Some people will never obtain the prize since they have not registered for the race. Their names are not recorded on the list of participants. Obviously, that is the first requirement that needs to be met in order to obtain the prize in the race. If you neither participate nor earnestly strive, you will certainly not obtain the prize.

Upon reaching the age of anywhere between eighteen and twenty-two, there comes a moment in your life when you must make a decision. Your peers are attending confession of faith class and are preparing themselves for public profession of faith. What will your decision be?

There are many who will not make profession of faith. They do not want to be obligated toward God and His Word. They wish to remain unattached and would prefer to practice Christianity and be religious without any strings attached. Obviously, they will not express themselves in such terms. Instead, they will say, "I do not wish to be a hypocrite," or "I will wait until I am ready for it." Or else one will say, "I am unconverted. In order to make profession of faith you must be converted. Thus, I will not make profession of faith."

These appear to be valid excuses for not making profession of faith. With the rare exception of those for whom this is a matter of conscience, the truth is that the majority of such are not interested in the race. The good fight of faith (cf. 1 Tim. 6:12; 2 Tim. 4:7) does not appeal to them.

Remember, however, that if your name has not yet been entered on the list of participants, you will not be able to obtain the prize. And if you do not obtain the prize of eternal life, you will receive the wages of sin, eternal death.

It will not suffice to be a spectator by either encouraging the runners in the race or criticizing them. It also will not suffice to make profession of faith as a matter of custom or to be rid of catechism instruction. You yourself must become a runner in the race of faith. Consider that there are but two ways: the narrow way that leads to eternal life, and the broad way that leads to destruction.

The call to make public profession of faith before God and the congregation will bring you into this dilemma. It is a must and yet you are not able. In this situation, only the prayer of the father remains from whom Jesus required something he could not do: "Lord, I believe, help thou mine unbelief."

Faith and Profession

The phrase *profession of faith* encompasses two concepts: *faith* and *to profess*. These two concepts clearly identify what making profession of faith is. The apostle writes, "If thou shalt confess with thy mouth the Lord Jesus, and shalt believe in thine heart that God hath raised him from the dead, thou shalt be saved" (Rom. 10:9). Faith in the heart is connected with the profession of the mouth.

Thus, faith and making profession are closely connected. Wherever there is fire, there will also be heat. When faith is present, there will also be a profession of this faith. You neither can nor may disconnect these two matters.

There are some who wish to believe without making a profession. One is then able to believe, even though he never speaks to others about it and never visits the church. Others wish to make a profession without believing. Is it not possible to make a profession without having faith? Is it not the main thing to be orthodox and sound in doctrine?

The point is, however, that faith and making profession belong together. Profession of faith is related in the first place to faith itself. Scripture speaks of "believing with the heart." Faith in the heart yields the profession of the mouth. The apostle therefore states, "I believed, and therefore have I spoken" (2 Cor. 4:13). Paul makes an appeal to the words of David from Psalm 116:10 in order to make clear why he preached the gospel and could not be silent about Christ. Paul believed the saving gospel of the Lord Jesus Christ, and therefore he spoke. There is a connection between the heart and the mouth. God cannot be pleased with a mere verbal profession without having faith in the heart. You will then only be Christian in name.

What does it mean to believe? In Hebrew, to believe means to say "Amen" in response to what someone else says. In the eastern context, one can never do this only intellectually, divorced from the heart. It always means more than merely "to acknowledge something to be true." To believe is a casting of one's entire being upon the promise.

It is within that context that faith is mentioned for the first time in Scripture. God promised to Abraham that He would make a great nation out of him and would bring forth the Messiah from him. Abraham responded in faith to this promise: "And he believed in the LORD; and he counted it to him for righteousness" (Gen. 15:6).

In the Old Testament, faith is to deem God trustworthy in His words and deeds, and to act accordingly. The issue is who God, by grace, desires to be for a sinner, and what He graciously will do. Faith responds to God's deeds and promises, and fully puts its trust in them. Faith always manifests itself as the act of a person who is in need, is stricken with guilt, and is helpless. The needy who have no helper are those who will put their trust in the Lord.

The Greek word for "to believe" is *pisteuo*. This also means that one deems God's Word trustworthy and fully relies upon it. Also in this instance we are dealing with more than an intellectual acknowledgment of the truth. It is a faith that delivers from God's wrath and results in a new manner of life.

The focus of the New Testament is primarily on faith in the saving acts of God in Christ. Christ is the object of faith who by His death on the cross has propitiated God and who by His resurrection has conquered death. Faith stands in connection with man's lost condition and his guilt, as well as with salvation in Christ as proclaimed by the gospel.

A believer is someone who is troubled about his sin, who fears death and eternity, who acknowledges his guilt before God, and who, in the midst of all this, trusts in God's promise that whosoever believes in a crucified Christ shall not perish but have eternal life. With his entire being, the sinner casts himself upon God's promise.

Faith implies, therefore, the acknowledgment of one's lost condition, but also a surrender and acceptance of God's salvation in Christ. John Owen defined faith as "the fleeing of a penitent sinner to the mercy of God in Christ."

This faith produces a profession. To profess (*homologia*) means to say exactly what God has said. It means that one publicly acknowledges this faith. Paul therefore says, "For I am not ashamed of the gospel of Christ" (Rom. 1:16).

That profession proceeds from faith. The act of faith, whereby one as a lost sinner entrusts himself to God and His grace in Christ, is in its very nature hidden and only known to God. It is a matter of the heart and only transpires between God and your heart. However, this hidden matter cannot remain hidden. A hidden faith becomes visible in its fruits. One professes what one believes.

This means that one will depart from his sinful ways and his lifeless religion. He will break with his former life. With heartfelt sorrow, he will bid farewell to sin and all evil. He will turn to the way of God's commandments and a new direction of life will be pursued. This is already a kind of profession of faith.

Profession with the mouth will also follow, however. Especially in the Acts of the Apostles, we can read what happens when one genuinely comes to faith in Christ.

As a result of the preaching of the Word, a sinner would see and believe who he was in the sight of God. He began to see how lost he was without God and Christ, which aroused a desire for the salvation and reconciliation proclaimed by the gospel. This led him to surrender himself wholly to the Christ who was preached. By this wholehearted surrender to Christ he found peace with God and deliverance from eternal death.

Consequently, he said farewell to a world destined for destruction and desired to enter the domain of Jesus Christ. He longed to be numbered among God's people, the congregation of Christ.

This required first of all a confession before the minister and the congregation. He would then be baptized and be received as a member of the body of Christ. Thus his inner faith became externally visible.

True faith cannot remain hidden. It needs to be confessed. God has spoken, you have believed it, and now your mouth cannot remain silent. The Lord Jesus said, "I tell you that, if these should hold their peace, the stones would immediately cry out" (Luke 19:40).

A faith is born within that cannot remain silent. When you have experienced who God is willing to be for a sinner, and you have become acquainted with Christ by faith, you will not be able to be silent about these things. The wonder of salvation is too great! "Out of the abundance of the heart the mouth speaketh" (Matt. 12:34).

God in Christ will then be confessed—in secret on your knees, at home, and in your extended family. You will also confess Him publicly; that is, at work and in the world, and especially in the midst of His congregation.

Thus, there is a connection between faith and the profession of this faith. Faith is the root and profession the fruit. The believer is a professing and witnessing believer. The church of Christ is a confessing church. "Whosoever therefore shall confess me before men, him will I confess also before my Father which is in heaven" (Matt. 10:32).

— 2 —
WHERE DOES THE PRACTICE OF MAKING PROFESSION OF FAITH ORIGINATE?

Profession of Faith in the Old Testament?

In the Old Testament you will not read anything about the practice of making profession of faith by children who have reached the age of maturity. This is probably due to children participating in the Passover and eating of the Passover lamb since their early youth. There is no mention of self-examination prior to the eating of the Passover lamb and the drinking of the wine at the Passover meal. However, we do read repeatedly that both young and old are exhorted to honor and serve the Lord with their whole heart. During a later period in Jewish history, some form of a personal profession by thirteen-year-old boys was in vogue. This would constitute a personal entering into covenant with God.

At the age of thirteen, a boy would be declared *bar mitzvah*, or a son of the law. After having been instructed by a rabbi, such a boy would be examined in order to demonstrate that he was capable of reading and expounding the law of God. On the Sabbath after his birthday, he would read from the Torah for the first time during a service in the synagogue.

From that moment on, he would be considered as someone who was responsible for his own actions and would be obliged to perform all the duties of a Jew. This circumcised Jew had now personally embraced the covenant and had become a son of the law.

A Jewish girl would automatically, without a special ceremony, become *bat mitzvah* at the age of twelve.

The Profession of Proselyte Baptism

Judaism did require some sort of a profession from Gentiles who requested incorporation into the Jewish congregation. The Gentile who desired to become a Jew, would first be informed by the Jewish authorities that Israel was subject to oppression and that it would therefore be wise to consider this prior to switching to Judaism.

If such a person insisted on becoming a Jew, he would be accepted into the Jewish community on a provisional basis and would be instructed in a number of religious regulations and duties. Among them were the ten commandments, the dietary laws, precepts concerning the observance of the Sabbath, etc.

Subsequent to this instruction, the men would be circumcised, then immersed into clean, transparent water. This signified the washing away of the pollution of being a Gentile. By means of this baptism, such a person would sever himself from his sinful and pagan past.

Prior to this baptism, he would have to denounce paganism and subscribe to the Jewish faith and its precepts. This transpired by way of what could be considered a public profession of faith, at which time he would have to recite the precepts and regulations of Judaism and make a solemn declaration that he would submit himself to them and be willing to observe them.

After the baptismal ceremony, the baptized person would be addressed with friendly words and be welcomed into the Jewish community. This would be followed by the offering of a sacrifice.

Gentile women were incorporated into Judaism in a similar fashion. They, however, were only baptized. This baptism would occur in the presence of Jewish women. The children were reckoned in their father and were considered as belonging to Judaism by way of baptismal immersion. They would thus be incorporated into God's covenant people.

The denunciation of paganism and the wholehearted acceptance of Jewish precepts were significant components of the transfer from paganism to Judaism.

The Profession Made at the Baptism of John

The baptism of John the Baptist was of great significance for Christianity of subsequent ages. The question pertaining to the origin of John's baptism was already an issue during Jesus' sojourn upon earth. The Pharisees, for fear of inciting public opinion against them, did not dare to say that this baptism was of man. Jesus taught that John's baptism was from heaven; it was God who had sent John to baptize. John the Baptist knew it to be his calling to prepare the way for the Messiah. To that end, he preached the baptism of repentance unto the remission of sins (Mark 1:4).

The origin of John's baptism is not to be found in proselyte baptism, but rather in God's commission. Its significance must undoubtedly be determined in light of Old Testament prophecies such as Ezekiel 36:25, Zechariah 13:1, and others. It must be viewed in connection with preparing a people for the Lord.

John's baptism demanded repentance and confession of sin, but also pointed to the forgiveness of sins through the Messiah who was about to come. As a result, John became the nucleus around which a new people of God gathered themselves, longing earnestly for the coming of the Messiah.

For us it is significant that John the Baptist did not baptize anyone unless he confessed his sins. By way of such a confession of sin, such a person acknowledged himself to be worthy of the very judgment John had pronounced. The ax was already at the root of the tree of the sinful nation of Israel.

On the other hand, this confession and submission to baptism was a profession of faith. The subject of baptism thereby expressed that he believed in John's preaching concerning the salvation to be accomplished by the coming Messiah. Therefore, the baptism of John was essentially identical in meaning to the baptism of the New Testament church. However, John did not baptize without the confession of guilt and faith.

Confession and Christian Baptism

It is evident that in the New Testament, confession and faith and baptism are inseparably linked together. The New Testament data concerning baptism do not leave us in doubt regarding this matter. Whenever the New Testament relates an administration of baptism, it always pertains to people who, with or without their families, have come to faith in Christ, and who confess this faith prior to their baptism (Acts 2:41).

In Samaria, Philip only baptized those who believed the gospel of the kingdom and name of Jesus Christ. This is clearly illustrated in the baptism of the eunuch. Philip would only baptize him if he believed with all his heart. In response, the eunuch made this confession: "I believe that Jesus Christ is the Son of God" (Acts 8:37). In this confession, we hear one of the first components of the apostolic confession.

The baptism of the eunuch has taken on great significance for the church. It yields a remarkable description of the work of the missionary church. Philip, the deacon, had been sent by God to the wilderness road of Gaza and encountered there a man who was reading the prophecy of Isaiah. The description of all the details of this event contains the elements of what would become the standard procedure of the missionary church. The prospective subject of baptism would first of all manifest his interest in God and the salvation of his soul. Subsequently, he would be instructed by pointing out to him, by way of the Old Testament Scriptures, that Jesus was the promised Messiah. This would transpire during a shorter or longer period of time. After such instruction, the pupil would express his desire to be baptized, upon which a personal profession of faith would be required. Upon such a profession of faith, both the teacher and the pupil would descend into the water, and the new convert would be baptized.

During the early history of the church, baptism was administered immediately after confession of faith and contrition. At that time, you do not yet read about instruction in Christian doctrine. The jailor of Philippi, Saul of Tarsus, the Corinthians, and the eunuch were all baptized without delay and without instruction.

However, when consulting the Didache (a document from the first century), there is reason to believe that early on, a period of instruction pertaining to the Christian faith was mandated prior to baptism. "As many as are convinced and believe that the things we teach and describe are true, and who promise to live accordingly, shall be instructed that they must pray and ask God, while fasting, for the forgiveness of sins. Then we shall bring them to a place where water is available and they shall then be born anew (baptized) in the same manner in which we also received the new birth; for they shall then be washed in water in the Name of the Father and the Lord God of all things, and of our Savior Jesus Christ, and of the Holy Ghost." The subject of baptism had to know the doctrine of Christ and believe it with his whole heart in order to be baptized. Baptism was then administered after confession of contrition as well as faith in Jesus. This would then yield the forgiveness of sins and the indwelling of the Holy Spirit. Subsequently, this person would then be received into the church and would be admitted to the Lord's Supper.

The sequence of events in the apostolic era was: confession of faith, baptism, and the Lord's Supper. This was also practiced in Samaria where Philip preached and baptized. Calvin relates the manner in which Philip proceeded: "Men and women could not be baptized without making confession of their faith; but they were admitted unto baptism upon this condition, that their families might be consecrated to God; for the covenant goeth thus: 'I will be thy God, and the God of thy seed'" (*Commentary* on Acts 8:12).

— 3 —
PROFESSION OF FAITH IN THE ANCIENT CHURCH

Confession of Faith and Believer's Baptism

Whoever desired to join the early Christian church would turn to an elder or deacon of the congregation. Accompanied by this elder as a witness, he would then, as a candidate for baptism, communicate this to the bishop. After an examination concerning his walk of life, a cross would be painted with oil on the forehead of the candidate for baptism and a probationary period would begin, during which this candidate would participate in congregational life. This probationary period would usually last three years. A candidate for baptism could, however, not partake of the Lord's Supper. He would then be asked to leave the service.

From the fourth century forward, the catechumen (students preparing for baptism) became a separate group in the church. The catechumen would be considered a *christianus* (Christian), but not yet a *fidelis* (believer) since he had not yet made profession of faith.

Upon completion of the probationary period, the candidate, together with the same witness, would again meet with the bishop to ask permission to be baptized. This would usually transpire nine or ten weeks prior to Easter. This visit would be followed by seven weeks of catechetical instruction. Five times during the week, the candidate would receive three hours of instruction. During the sixth week, profession of faith would be made. This profession would be repeated during the seventh week and consisted of the recital of the twelve articles of the Apostles' Creed. On Easter morning, after having made profession of faith once more, he would be baptized, and a week later he would partake of the Lord's Supper for the first time.

This teaches us how much attention was given to preparing for making profession of faith. It was viewed as a thoroughly prepared and tested profession of both the mouth and the heart. Profession of faith and believer's baptism were inseparably connected.

The profession required prior to being baptized as a believer was enlarged during the course of time. The candidate for baptism, while standing in the water, would renounce his allegiance to the devil. This was followed by a three-fold pouring of water on the person, and a profession of faith would precede each dispersion of water. Prior to each dispersion of water, a question would be asked, upon which the person would have to answer with, "I believe." The first time one would ask, "Do you believe in God almighty, Creator of heaven and earth?" The second question would be, "Do you believe in Jesus Christ, His only begotten Son, our Lord, who was born, crucified, and rose again?" The third question was, "Do you believe in the Holy Ghost, the forgiveness of sins, eternal life, and the holy church?" This resulted in the formulation of a permanent baptismal profession of faith.

Upon emerging from the water, the baptismal candidate would be anointed in the name of Christ, just as Moses anointed Aaron. This would symbolize the blessings which one had received by way of baptism. This was followed by a solemn laying on of hands and a symbolic communication of God's blessing, as well as the eating of milk and honey in order to be strengthened.

Next, the baptized persons were clothed with a white baptismal garment which pointed to the acquired purification through Christ's blood and the duty to walk in newness of life. This would be followed by placing the mark of the cross upon the forehead as a symbol of fellowship with Christ, and frequently there would also be a second anointing with oil. After this, they could call themselves a believer and partake of the Lord's Supper.

Profession of Faith at Infant Baptism

Infant baptism became the common practice very early in church history. From statements made by Tertullianus (200 A.D.), we know that infant baptism was already then the established practice of the church. Origin states that infant baptism was the common practice during his days, and Cyprian concurs with this. The Council of Carthage (256 A.D.) decreed that baptism should be administered already on the second or third day after birth.

When the church became established (approximately 450 A.D.), infant baptism gradually became the rule and believer's baptism the exception. The church was not only growing as a result of the Gentiles joining the church, but also because children of believers remained with the church.

There was a period of time, however, when many would still postpone baptism; only think of Augustine. However, infant baptism increasingly became the established practice. This was especially precipitated by the fact that during the sixth century, after the influx of many new converts, few people from heathendom embraced the Christian faith. The Christian church deemed the line of God's covenant with the Jewish people to be extended into the church. It is particularly noteworthy that during this period, when discussing infant baptism, frequent references are made to Noah and his family and the flood, circumcision, and the crossing of the Red Sea.

The emergence of infant baptism as common practice changed the historical sequence of profession of faith, baptism, and the Lord's Supper. Profession of faith became the link between the two sacraments and the sequence became baptism, profession of faith, and the Lord's Supper.

The question arose how this should be dealt with when baptizing infants. The church wanted to maintain the organic connection between infant baptism and believer's baptism. After all, it was the same baptism; the only problem was that little children were not able to speak. This was also the case with those who were deaf-mutes. Others would then represent them and make profession of faith for them.

Likewise, parents or god-parents would be able to make profession of faith for the child who was not yet of age. They would speak and act on behalf of the child and in his or her name, recite the twelve articles, and perform the *abrenuntiatio* (the solemn renouncing of allegiance to Satan). Matters that the child was not yet able to perform were performed by the parents. In this manner, the organic unity of profession, faith, and baptism was maintained.

Believer's baptism had to be preceded by catechetical instruction, whereas instruction had to follow infant baptism. The parents or the godparents were not absolved of their responsibility by representing the child at baptism. They would be obliged to instruct the child or to have him or her instructed by someone else. This resulted in the emergence of catechetical instruction.

After being baptized as a child, one would be catechized by the church in preparation for a subsequent public profession of faith and partaking of the Lord's Supper. By way of a personal profession of faith, the child would have to become a believer and thereby obtain admittance to the Lord's Supper.

Augustine already made mention of this. He deemed the faith of the parents or sponsors only representative for the child as long as the child was not of age. When the child would come to the years of discretion, he would have to learn to understand the significance of his baptism, and also be urged to embrace it.

Baptized children were not yet able "to believe with the heart and to confess with the mouth." As long as this was not the case, baptism was deemed to be efficacious to preserve the child from the power of the devil, and if the child were to die at an early age, he or she would be saved in Christ. The promises of God were not considered contingent upon the faith of the individual. It was Augustine's view that "baptized children, by their crying, frequently drown out the words of the promises of God, and yet God desires to be their God."

The adult person, however, needed a personal faith in God's promises to be saved. Baptism was therefore never an end in and of itself; that which was sealed in the sacraments needed to be followed by the conversion of the heart and a personal faith. "The sacrament of baptism is one thing, and the conversion of the heart another, but the salvation of man consists of the union of both" (*Augustinus De baptismo*, IV, 25).

Such was the teaching concerning the necessity of a personal profession of faith by those who were baptized as children.

Confirmation
The same thing transpired at both infant baptism and believer's

baptism, with the exception that the parents or sponsors would answer for the child. At a later date, the child would be required to make a personal profession of faith and publicly embrace his baptism. Children were baptized on the basis of this principle.

The church taught that by answering the questions on behalf of the child, the parents or godparents would enter into a spiritual relationship with the baptized child.

At baptism, the bishop would ask, "Do you forsake the devil and all his works?" The godfather would then answer on behalf of the child, "I do forsake!" The bishop would then proceed to ask, "Do you desire to be baptized?" Again the godparents would answer affirmatively on behalf of the child. After reading the twelve articles, the bishop would ask three times, "Do you believe?", upon which the godparents would respond, "*Credo*, I believe."

It was evident that the child himself was not yet capable of making profession of faith, and thus others would do it for the child. These persons would enter into a special relationship with the child and bear responsibility for the child's Christian upbringing.

When the church became increasingly Roman Catholic, drifting away from the teaching of Scripture, the public profession of faith made by baptized persons was transformed into a sacrament.

At first, the laying on of hands and the anointing with oil took place at the baptism of children, but these practices were later transferred to the profession of faith of baptized persons. During the thirteenth century, both the laying on of hands and the anointing with oil were elevated to a sacrament. This was called the sacrament of confirmation, and later it was simply called "confirmation." The reason for this lies in the fact that when making profession of faith, a person would be marked with anointing oil on the forehead in the sign of the cross, while the following words were pronounced, "I mark you with the symbol of the cross and confirm you with the oil of salvation, in the name of the Father, the Son, and the Holy Ghost."

Baptism was administered by the local pastor, whereas confirmation was administered by the bishop. He would lay his hands upon the young people as a symbol of having the Holy Spirit communicated to them. He would anoint them, mark them with the mark of the cross, and would then offer prayer.

It was not very long before this transaction became a sacrament called confirmation, whereby grace is communicated. The word "confirmation" is derived from the application of the anointing oil by which the mark of the cross (*chrisma*) was made, as well as from the formula (*forma*) which was recited.

Thus, confirmation is a sacrament whereby, upon the laying on of hands, the anointing with *chrisma*, and the prayer of the bishop, the recipient would receive grace to remain steadfast in the faith.

By way of the sacrament of confirmation, a person would be molded and equipped to be a soldier in Christ's army. He would thereby receive the spiritual weapons as well as the strength to battle Satan, the world, and sin. Confirmation was a mark of identification with Christ.

At the same time, there was a move toward making profession of faith at an earlier age. Already at the age of twelve or thirteen people would be confirmed; this now occurs at the age of seven.

Catechetical instruction was given less and less frequently, and the practice of a probationary period, coupled with an examination of both life and doctrine, disappeared entirely. This resulted from a shift of emphasis from profession of faith to the receiving of the sacrament. People no longer came forward to make public profession of faith, but to receive, by way of the sacrament, grace for leading a pious life.

In 1274, the Council of Lyon decreed confirmation to be a sacrament. It thereby became of the same import as baptism and the Lord's Supper. In fact, in one sense, confirmation had even greater significance than baptism and the Lord's Supper, as the latter were administered by ordinary priests. The sacrament of confirmation, however, could only be administered by the bishop. As a result, the church esteemed her own institution to be of greater import than the institutions of Christ. This was an obvious characteristic of the future Roman Catholic Church.

Thus, grace was communicated by the act of confirmation. The sacrament of confirmation made a person fit for the receipt of the grace of God in Christ. One did not profess the grace of God he had become acquainted with in Christ, but rather came forward to receive this grace by way of the sacrament. In fact, this Roman

Catholic confirmation is not a profession of faith, but a sacramental infusion of grace unto faith and the perseverance in faith.

Since the transmission of grace in baptism was insufficient, it was confirmed and complemented by way of confirmation. God's grace in baptism was complemented by way of the sacrament of the church.

— 4 —
Profession of Faith in the Reformation

Opposition to Infant Baptism
Although Luther and Calvin rejected the notion that confirmation was a sacrament, all the Reformers sought to maintain a connection with the tradition of the early church. Thus, baptized children had to be instructed and, upon completion of such instruction, make a conscious confession of the faith which their parents or godparents had confessed at their baptism. The fact remained that the biblical order is faith, profession, and baptism.

The Anabaptists did not cease to confront the Reformers with this by saying that children may not be baptized since they cannot confess their faith. Today we hear the same arguments from Baptists, charismatic groups, and others. Time and again they will challenge us with the fact that faith must first be present. Without faith, one cannot benefit from the sacraments. Frequently they will say to us, "If you do not admit young children to the Lord's Supper, then why do you admit them to baptism?"

The Reformers responded to the Anabaptists by pointing first of all to the difference between baptism and the Lord's Supper. Baptism is the sacrament of regeneration, whereas the Lord's Supper is the sacrament of continual nourishment. For the sacrament of the Lord's Supper, self-examination is mandatory; however, this is not true for baptism. Furthermore, baptism is a sign and seal of the covenant of grace and not a sign of faith. It is not a confirmation that someone possesses faith, but rather a seal upon God's covenant and promises.

In his *Institutes*, Calvin dismantles at least twenty arguments which Servetus had advanced against infant baptism. Baptism confirms God's covenant and promises to the children of the congregation. The church may not permit herself to be robbed of this comfort, whatever the arguments may be. "It is precisely this which

Satan is attempting in assailing infant baptism with such an army: that, once this testimony of God's grace is taken away from us, the promise which, through it, is put before our eyes may eventually vanish little by little" (*Institutes*, 4.16.32). How true these words have proven to be! Among those who are opposed to infant baptism, the notion of the covenant of grace is frequently entirely absent. They have lost sight of God's covenant and its promises. Frequently, they only focus on what the believer promises in baptism and not on what God promises in and by way of baptism. The sight of the magnificent message of God's covenant faithfulness in the generations has been lost. For that very reason the Reformers did not want to dispense with infant baptism.

However, that does not mean that they lost sight of the relationship between profession of faith and baptism. Being baptized as a child had to be followed by a personal profession of faith. "So soon as the capacity of their age shall suffer, they may addict themselves to be His [Christ's] disciples" (Calvin's *Commentary* on Acts 8:36-37).

In this manner, children would become mature members of the congregation. Everyone would have to give a personal account of his faith before the rights and privileges of the church would be his as an adult member. In the Reformation, profession of faith was rooted in baptism. Already then the child should have confessed his or her faith.

Luther's Views

Luther insisted upon having a special ceremony to mark the conclusion of the instruction given to the youth of the church. This was referred to as confirmation or profession of faith. Though Luther rejected confirmation as a sacrament, the name "confirmation" remained in use for the ecclesiastical ceremony of profession of faith. The completion of ecclesiastical instruction would be followed by what could be called an examination of personal faith, upon which one would make profession of faith and be admitted to the Lord's Supper.

There was a close relationship between profession of faith and the Lord's Supper. Anyone who wished to be admitted to the Lord's Supper had to come to the minister for a further examination of his doctrine and to make profession of faith. Upon examination, one would have to prove that he possessed sufficient knowledge for the proper celebration of the Lord's Supper and make a statement that it was his desire to partake of the Lord's Supper in the proper manner, namely, out of love for Christ and without living in disharmony with his neighbor.

This examination would be repeated annually at the beginning of his membership, and would be conducted again at stated times during the course of his life. Later, this was replaced with public examination in the church in the presence of the congregation.

This examination pertained to the three components of Christian doctrine: the trio of misery, deliverance, and gratitude; the doctrine of the sacraments; and the doctrine of the keys of the kingdom of heaven. Thus, the emphasis was shifted more and more toward something that could be called an ecclesiastical examination. If one would successfully pass this, the way to the Lord's table would be open.

Making profession of faith was considered a sequel to infant baptism. Luther, in responding to the view of the Anabaptists that children cannot believe and thus cannot be baptized, defended himself by the view of the early church. "Here I say what all say, that a *fides aliena* (an alien faith, that is, faith in Another, even Jesus Christ) assists those small children."

Parents professed faith instead of the child and took responsibility for it. Later Reformers fully embraced this thought, namely, that parents or godparents make profession on behalf of the children. You will find this in our form for the administration for baptism, by requiring an answer to the question, "Whether you acknowledge the doctrine which is contained in the Old and New Testaments, and in the articles of the Christian faith, and which is taught here in this Christian church, to be the true and perfect doctrine of salvation?"

We also recognize this in the question, "Whether you promise and intend to see these children, when come to the years of discretion (whereof you are either parent or witness), instructed and brought up in the aforesaid doctrine, or help or cause them to be instructed therein, to the utmost of your power?" The phrase "promise and intend" means therefore "to assume responsibility for."

This *fides aliena* does not mean that one can believe on someone's behalf. Upon reaching maturity, the child himself must believe personally and make profession of faith. By insisting on this, Luther wished to maintain the relationship between faith and Baptism. The baptized child must make a personal profession of his faith; only this opens the door to all the blessings of the church, and especially to the Lord's Supper.

Luther even entertained the notion of a "baptism congregation" and a "Lord's Supper congregation." In the church-at-large, a pure core of true believers would gather around the Lord's table. The "Lord's Supper congregation" would be subject to a much stricter form of church discipline and constitute the true, Christian church. Luther was never able to put this idea into practice. He did teach, however, that one needed a personal profession of faith as well as experience of faith to belong to the true people of God, the congregation of Christ.

Calvin's Views

Calvin primarily embraced the views of Martin Bucer. This meant that whoever desired to partake of the Lord's Supper needed to first make profession of faith. Bucer wrote, "They must have the marks of the regenerate and have come to Christian maturity."

After having been instructed in the doctrines of the church, the baptized members would make a personal profession of faith, whereby the ministers would install their catechumens (confirmation) as mature members of the congregation. This confirmation occurred by way of an ecclesiastical ceremony which bore much resemblance to the traditions of the early church. In church, the young people would have to respond publicly to eighteen questions, and thereafter the twelve articles of faith would be recited. With a solemn "yes" they would promise to persevere in maintaining fellowship with the church, to embrace the preaching by faith, to obey the exhortations of the office-bearers to amend their life, and to subject themselves to the discipline of the church.

After prayer, there would be a solemn laying on of hands and the ceremony would be concluded with the words, "May you receive the Holy Spirit, protection against all evil, and strength and help to perform all that is good from the gracious hand of the Father, Son, and Holy Spirit, Amen."

Thus Calvin, emulating Bucer, also aligned himself with the tradition of the early church. His criticism of confirmation must not be viewed as opposition to a public confession of faith with the laying on of hands, but rather to the degeneration of this meaningful, apostolic practice to some sort of complementary sacrament. He was much in favor of including the laying on of hands as an affirmation of public profession of faith. For the baptized children of the church, there needed to be an ecclesiastical ceremony whereby they could profess their faith which they had not confessed at baptism. There had to be a specific procedure in the church to conclude catechetical instruction and to open the door to the Lord's table.

The church was obliged to lead baptized members to confession of faith. This had to be the focus of the entire training of the parents and the catechetical instruction of the church. Calvin strongly emphasized Christian child-rearing by parents and the catechetical instruction of the church as a means to guide baptized children to a public profession of the only true and genuine faith.

For Calvin, catechetical instruction has three objectives:

(1) Baptized children must be led to make a personal profession of faith. They are obligated to do so by virtue of their baptism. That faith of which they could not give an account at their baptism, they must publicly confess when they reach maturity, "by which we publicly confess that we wish to be reckoned God's people" (*Institutes*, 4.15.13). Thus, Calvin desired to align himself completely with the tradition of the early church. Those who had been baptized as infants, because they had not made confession of faith before the church, were again presented by their parents at the end of their childhood or at the beginning of adolescence, and were examined by the bishop according to the form of the catechism (*Institutes*, 4.19.4). In essence, one should have made profession of faith at baptism. Baptized children are not exempt from this duty; baptism obligates one to make profession of faith. God's covenant must be embraced. Viewed as such, profession of faith is an act of obedience toward

God's covenant, of which baptism is a sign and a seal. Calvin deemed it desirable that baptized children, at the age of fifteen or sixteen, would confirm the confession their parents made at their baptism; four times a year he granted the opportunity to do so in connection with the administration of the Lord's Supper. Thus we observe that, for Calvin, there is an obvious relationship between baptism, profession of faith, and the Lord's Supper.

Calvin did not examine the state of a person's heart. He did consistently maintain, however, that a person's faith must be more than external knowledge. The catechism instructor must therefore not only instruct his catechumen (teach them), but also urge his catechumens to believe in Christ (pastor them). In this pastoral aspect of his work, he had to impress upon the children the necessity of the experience of the Christian faith. The doctrines of the church had to be embraced by faith.

For Calvin, the thrust of the instruction of the youth is primarily toward making public profession of faith—and specifically, on a profession of the heart. Baptized members must learn to believe with their heart in order to be able to profess with their mouth. This theme surfaces repeatedly. The objective of this instruction must not only be the acquisition of knowledge, but also the eternal salvation of the children.

(2) A person must know what he professes. A faith of the heart has content—namely, God's truth as confessed and taught by the church. Calvin deemed the knowledge of faith to be very important, for there is no faith without true knowledge. Knowledge and faith are inseparably united. However, he did not merely stress intellectual knowledge, but rather the believing knowledge of the truth.

(3) Catechetical instruction is essential for the preservation of the truth. The members of the church must be able to give an account of their faith. The truth must be transmitted from father to child. "Teachers are…put in charge…only of scriptural interpretation — to keep the doctrine whole and pure among believers" (*Institutes*, 4.3.4). The church would not be troubled as much by error if one would be able to discern between truth and error.

Profession of Faith in the Reformed Churches of the Netherlands

The Dutch churches followed Calvin's example in catechizing baptized members and in requiring public profession of faith. They greatly emphasized a knowledge of the doctrines of Scripture, but also a faith of the heart.

Much attention was given to training children in the doctrines of Christianity. As to the training of children, godparents were not to assume the place of the parents. At home, in the schools, and in the church, children needed to be trained so that they might correctly understand and experience the reality of their baptism.

The objective of child rearing and catechetical instruction needed to be the guidance of baptized members toward a personal and public profession of their faith. As early as the Convent of Wesel (1568), the Reformed churches expressed by this view that they desired to align themselves with the tradition of the early church and the apostles, "since it had been transmitted to them by the apostles and their followers."

There was an intimate connection between profession of faith and the Lord's Supper. They embraced the following sequence: birth to believing parents, infant baptism, catechetical instruction, a voluntary and public profession of faith, and thereafter admission to the Lord's Supper. This is evident from the rulings of the Convent of Wesel (1568). There it was stipulated what would later be codified in the 1618-19 Church Order of Dort: "No one should be admitted to the Lord's Supper unless he has first made a profession of faith and shall have submitted himself to ecclesiastical discipline" (*Articles of Wesel*, 6:7-11). Eight days prior to the celebration of the Lord's Supper, all who desired to partake of it would have to meet with the minister. Inquiries would then be made regarding one's walk of life. If the outcome was satisfactory, the prospective members would be questioned regarding their knowledge of doctrine and personal life of faith. In this manner, oversight was exercised over doctrine and life, but also over the motives prompting one to request admission to the Lord's Supper.

With young people, profession of faith would always be preceded by a designated period of catechetical instruction, whereafter one would be examined about his knowledge of the doctrines. This examination would usually be conducted in the congregation. Subsequently, the matter of personal faith would be addressed in a smaller gathering. Eight days prior to the administration of the Lord's Supper, one would then make profession of faith in the midst of the congregation.

The Convent of Wesel expressed itself as follows: "However, it should not be deemed strange that those young people who have completed their catechetical instruction be examined before the entire congregation according to the form of the large catechism, and that this be done eight days prior to the administration of the Lord's Supper. One shall set before them the most significant articles of the faith in order that they might acquiesce in them. At the same time, they shall submit themselves to ecclesiastical discipline and their names shall be recorded in the membership register. Then, after having informed the congregation and if there are no objections, they shall on a subsequent day be admitted to the Lord's Supper" (*Articles of Wesel*, 6:10-11). At the renowned National Synod of Dort, the issue of the profession of faith of baptized children was also discussed. First, thorough instruction in the doctrines was deemed to be essential. The Synod decreed "that catechetical instruction should be given in a three-fold manner, so that the Christian youth, beginning with their tender years, might diligently be instructed in the fundamentals of true religion and may be filled with true godliness."

Young people were to be instructed in a three-fold manner:

(1) at home by the parents;

(2) in school by the teachers;

(3) in the churches by the ministers, elders and readers, or visitors of the sick.

At the beginning of the Reformation, the congregations consisted primarily of a small number of professing members and a large number of baptized members. Baptized members did not always make profession of faith, as discipline was strictly administered.

The focus was not merely on a certain measure of knowledge and a personal faith, but especially upon a Christian walk. The consistory would carefully observe whether a person's profession was accompanied by a blameless walk. If one was a professing member and did not live according to God's Word, he could count on being subjected to church discipline and being refused admittance to the Lord's Supper. Consequently, the number of professing members in the congregation would be relatively small and the number of baptized members large. The baptized members who faithfully frequented the church but did not yet proceed to make profession of faith, became a separate group in the church. They were designated as "lovers of the truth."

Some church attendees would faithfully frequent the church their entire lives without making profession of faith. They did so either because they lacked liberty to partake of the Lord's Supper, or because they considered the administration of discipline too strict and would rather have more freedom in their way of life.

The Practice of the Dutch Second Reformation
(*Nadere Reformatie*)

The number of professing members increased in proportion to the transformation of the Reformed church to a state church. The government did not permit a very strict administration of discipline. Everyone should be able to be a member of the church. Strict stipulations which would inhibit church membership were not permitted to be formulated. Many became professing members who were ignorant of the doctrine and did not live in harmony with God's Word. In many congregations, there was a sad state of affairs regarding a knowledge of the truth and consequently the absence of godly life. Becoming a professing member became a meaningless formality.

During the time of the Reformation, it had been dangerous to be a subscriber to the new doctrine; the stakes were smoking. However, it had now become an honor to be a member of the Reformed church. Whoever aspired to political office had to be a member of the church. It is understandable, therefore, that many joined the church without having inner convictions. No matter how little one's knowledge was, consistories would rarely reject anyone. Koelman informs us that many ministers shamefully neglected the much needed catechetical instruction. However, there were always some ministers who took catechetical instruction seriously and who made a godly life requisite for making profession of faith. They taught the necessity of self-examination before attending the Lord's Supper.

The men of the Dutch Second Reformation were very conscious of the pitfalls of a national church, and observed with much concern that many professing members lacked knowledge and a sanctified walk. They sought to adhere to the old, Reformed view that making profession of faith requires knowledge of doctrine, self-examination in regard to the Lord's Supper, and a godly walk. However, they did not wish to be the judge of someone's heart. They put much emphasis upon domestic and public life. If this was not in harmony with God's Word, one would be barred from the Lord's table.

Though they did not judge the heart, they did teach what sort of faith was necessary in order to partake of the Lord's Supper. They were more careful to guard the Lord's table than to examine one's profession of faith. One was required to examine himself whether he did possess true faith. True faith could be identified by certain marks and was distinguished from all counterfeit faith. For the comfort of struggling believers, ministers would enumerate in their preaching the many marks of true faith, seeking at the same time to expose the hypocrites by showing the great difference between a true saving faith and a historical and temporal faith.

However, an unintended result of this was that the relationship between making profession of faith and the Lord's Supper became less firm. In localities where preaching was not very searching, all professing members would simply come to the Lord's table, while in more orthodox congregations, an increasing number of professing members would not partake.

Later Developments

During the nineteenth century, this development accelerated. Particularly in the churches of the Secession, more attention was given to the Lord's table than to making profession of faith. In some congregations, it became customary to partake of the Lord's Supper once after making profession of faith, and thereafter one would no longer partake. In other congregations, profession of faith was completely disconnected from the Lord's Supper. The threshold for making profession of faith became increasingly lower, and the threshold to the Lord's table increasingly higher. Thus we observe a shift in the relationship between baptism, profession of faith, and the Lord's Supper.

For instance, when considering the practice of Willem Teellinck's days (1579-1629), we must conclude that many made profession of faith and many partook of the Lord's Supper. He says concerning this, "that in every church many hundreds, and in some churches more than a thousand people would come to the table of the Lord."

However, in the congregation of Schortinghuis, at the beginning of the eighteenth century, the situation was entirely different. In the congregation of Midwolda, with fifteen hundred members, about twenty persons were permitted to make public profession of faith during the sixteen years that Schortinghuis ministered there. Undoubtedly, this was an exception, for Schortinghuis demanded that a person would be able to produce evidences of regeneration before he could make profession. Nevertheless, it was an indication that circumstances had changed.

At the beginning of the Reformation, only few made profession of faith and only few came to the Lord's table. In the emerging state church of the seventeenth century, however, it was common that everyone made profession of faith and came to the Lord's table. Later, around the time of the Secession, only few among the orthodox made profession of faith, but then would not come to the Lord's table.

The age at which a person would make profession of faith also changed. During the time of the Reformation, profession was made at the young age of fifteen or sixteen. This shifted toward eighteen years of age, and in some areas one would only make profession at a later age—the latter in connection with coming to the Lord's table.

The common practice in orthodox churches today is that you must have reached the age of maturity, twenty years of age being average.

Nevertheless, the matter of making profession of faith is being reexamined during recent years. A strong connection has again been established between making profession of faith and the Lord's Supper. In such churches, a person waits with making profession of faith until he has a desire to partake of the Lord's Supper and is a possessor of grace as stipulated in the questions for self-examination in the form for the administration of the Lord's Supper. In these churches, there is a return to the former situation of few professing members who all partake of the Lord's Supper, and many baptized members who only frequent the church services.

Others, however, have made a strong separation between making profession of faith and the Lord's Supper. Making profession of faith is more a profession of the truth than of personal faith. If one agrees with the doctrine and lives a blameless life, the way to making profession of faith is made easy for him. Professing members are often not asked why they do not come to the Lord's table. It is common that most professing members do not come to the Lord's table, whereas partaking of the Lord's table is unusual.

Finally, there is also a middle road which is followed by most orthodox churches. Making profession of faith is viewed as a personal choice by young people to join themselves to the congregation of the Lord and to take over the responsibility for their baptism from their parents. The relationship between making profession of faith and the Lord's Supper is recognized, but, at the same time, it is expressly taught for whom the Lord's Supper is instituted. In reality, however, this means that the threshold to the Lord's table is rather high, so that only a few members of the church partake of the Lord's Supper.

The sequence of the trio of baptism, profession of faith, and the Lord's Supper is still preferred for these churches. The church, however, does not know the heart and may not judge its state. Therefore, oversight is exercised only in regard to doctrine and life when profession of faith is made. Thereafter, a professing member is instructed in the preparatory sermon as to what is needed to partake of the Lord's Supper rightly. Following in the footsteps of the Dutch Second Reformation, more attention is given to the Lord's Supper than to making profession of faith.

In the meantime, all these differing opinions have caused a great deal of confusion and do generate many questions. Following this historical survey, I will address these questions.

— 5 —
Profession of Faith and Baptism

Baptism was the preeminent sacrament of the early church. During the period of the first Christians and the early church fathers, people were incorporated into the Christian church by baptism. The administration of baptism was always preceded by a personal profession of faith, for a sacrament is only meaningful when faith is present. Candidates for baptism knew and professed Christian doctrine, and they made a personal profession of this. In that context we hear the eunuch confess, "I believe that Jesus Christ is the Son of God" (Acts 8:37).

Such a personal profession of faith does not occur when children are baptized, for the child is not capable of making such a profession. However, the child that has been born of Christian parents does belong to the Christian church by virtue of birth. The children of Christians are not unclean heathens; they are "holy." The apostle expresses this: "Else were your children unclean; but now are they holy" (1 Cor. 7:14).

In light of this fact, the church began baptizing infants at a very early date—earlier than can be researched. The church saw God's covenant of grace not only in the Old, but also in the New Testament. If children were comprehended in God's covenant in the Old Testament, then this was certainly also true in the New Testament. If God's covenant and promises also pertain to them, as Peter declares on the day of Pentecost (Acts 2:39), the sign of the covenant pertains to them as well.

Why should children be deprived of that which God expressly prescribed for the children of Israel? Is not the essence of the covenant identical in both the old and new covenant? Christ was the great content of the promises of the old covenant, and He is also the essence of the fulfillment of the new covenant. The early church emulated Paul in referring to baptism as the circumcision of Christ

(Col. 2:11-12). God's covenant pertains to believers and their seed. It is one of the essential features of the covenant of grace that it also pertains to succeeding generations. When God established His covenant with Abraham, his descendants were also comprehended in this, for the Lord said He would "be a God unto thee and to thy seed after thee" (Gen. 17:7).

Our form for the administration of baptism states that whatever the Lord once said to Abraham is presently also addressed to us: "…and therefore unto us and our children, saying, 'I will establish my covenant between Me and thee, and thy seed after thee, in their generations, for an everlasting covenant.'" The truth that God has comprehended the seed of believers in His covenant can be found throughout the Scriptures.

Concerning the difficulties confronting us when examining the biblical data, I only wish to say that there are two kinds of covenant children, and that all Israel is not Israel. It is ultimately God's electing grace which makes a distinction among the children of men. Thus, Jacob and Esau were covenant children in different senses of the word.

Indeed, we may join the Heidelberg Catechism in saying, concerning our children, that "they, as well as the adult, are included in the covenant and church of God" (Q & A 74). Since they are comprehended in the covenant of grace, the sign of the covenant, holy baptism, also pertains to them.

Nevertheless, how do we deal with the profession of faith which preceded each administration of baptism in the early church?

Baptism Obligates One to Make Profession of Faith

Since an infant cannot make a personal profession of faith at baptism, we have concluded earlier that the parents do so on behalf of the child. In response to the third question, they have committed themselves to "see these children instructed…or help or cause them to be instructed." At that moment, the parents assumed responsibility for this profession.

This does not mean, however, that baptized children are absolved from the responsibility of making a personal profession of faith. Upon reaching adulthood, you are called to make a personal profession of faith and embrace your baptism. Then your personal responsibility becomes a factor and you are called to respond to what God has done in and by means of baptism. Thus, your obligation to make profession of faith is rooted in your baptism.

God's covenant obligates one to make profession of faith. As baptized children grow older, they must learn to understand the significance of baptism as a sign of the covenant, as well as embrace their baptism personally. Calvin puts it this way: "They must make profession of the faith to which they could not bear testimony at their baptism" (*Institutes*, 4.19.4). The church has asked for this at the baptism of the child by praying, "that they then may acknowledge Thy fatherly goodness and mercy which Thou hast shown to them and us."

It is an answer to prayer for the praying congregation when young people embrace their baptism and make a personal profession of faith. Therefore, true saints rejoice when young people align themselves with the congregation by way of profession of faith. Though we do not know the heart, we may nevertheless observe in this the Lord's care for, and faithfulness toward, the rising generation.

Thus, making profession of faith is primarily connected with baptism and not first and foremost with the Lord's Supper. I believe that we often lose sight of this. Our baptism obligates us to make profession of faith. By way of baptism, a triune God has established His claim upon your life. You are called to profess His name—and the Lord demands a profession of the heart. Whatever you believe with your heart, you must confess.

Must you then wait with making profession of faith until you know that you are a partaker of grace? You would then at least be able to make a heart profession and subsequently partake of the Lord's Supper. However, such reasoning would enable you to escape the demand to profess your faith—a demand to which baptism obligates you. God neither can nor will permit you to do this. This demand is inescapable. You are no longer neutral, for you are already a member of the Christian church. At your baptism, it was confessed, "...and therefore as members of His church ought to be baptized."

The question therefore is, "Do you accept this fact, or do you reject it?"

Profession of Faith and Baptism

Regarding an organization you can say, "I will become a member," or "I do not wish to become a member." We are here dealing, however, with an entirely different matter. Due to God's gracious providence, you have already been incorporated into the church, and as you grow older, the call comes to you, "Choose ye this day whom ye will serve" (Josh. 24:15).

There comes a time that, as a baptized member, you can no longer be reckoned in your parents. You must then personally make a choice. It will be one or the other: Your membership in God's church by virtue of birth and baptism must either be terminated, or you must extend your membership by making profession of faith. In either case, you make a choice, for by not making a choice, you are also making a choice. You can never remain neutral toward the Lord and His service. It will always be a matter of *for* or *against*!

The well-known Rev. Bernardus Smytegelt, in a sermon about baptism, addresses young people who do not wish to make profession of faith by saying, "If you have no desire to serve the Lord, be honest enough to come forward and disown your baptism in front of the pulpit!"

God's gracious direction, which brought you within the confines of the covenant of grace, confronts you with a great responsibility with which you must deal. You are called either to embrace God's covenant or to reject it. Embracing God's covenant is not the same as saying, "I choose for Jesus!" It is also not the same as saying, "Now I believe that I am a child of God." There is only one way in which one can embrace God's covenant: in the way of repentance and faith.

Repentance or conversion must take place. There must be a heartfelt return to God from whom you have departed and against whom you have sinned. Faith must be exercised. With your great need and all your guilt, you must turn to God and the gospel message of salvation in Christ.

There are many who claim that this is not necessary for a baptized person. They maintain that by baptism you are already a partaker of all things, having become a recipient of this in the promise of baptism. All you need to do is to embrace this. In this manner, however, the necessity of regeneration, repentance, and a personal faith in Christ is negated.

Others will say that you cannot convert yourself and that you must therefore wait until God converts you. The necessity of repentance and faith is no longer viewed as a duty, but rather is expressed as a wish. It absolves you from all responsibility, for "there is nothing you can do about it anyway," they say. As a result, there will be no striving to enter in at the narrow gate.

Thus, there are many ways in which the necessity of repentance toward God and a personal faith in Christ is neutralized. However, God proclaims to you, "Repent, and believe the gospel." You must repent; that is, with a sorrowful heart you must turn away from all known sin and turn in faith to God who is gracious in Christ. God offers the covenant, with all its treasures and blessings, to sinners who are subject to the curse of the broken covenant of works, proclaiming, "Incline your ear, and come unto me: hear, and your soul shall live; and I will make an everlasting covenant with you, even the sure mercies of David" (Isa. 55:3).

Tell me, what is your response to this? Let me conclude with a quote from the well-known book of Thomas Boston, *The Covenant of Grace*: "Thus the covenant has been brought near and presented to you in the gospel, so that you must of necessity either embrace it or reject it. Do not reject it, for this is more dangerous than can be expressed. Take hold of it, for your life is at stake!"

May this bring you into a bind. If you withdraw yourself from this responsibility, whatever your pious pretense may be, you will demonstrate that you have no regard for God's covenant. Then God's righteous covenant wrath will be executed upon you. On the other hand, if you make profession of faith purely out of custom and only with your mind, you will also not be blessed. A confession with the mouth is not sufficient. A confessed faith must also be an experienced faith. Calvin says regarding this: "We may not hide behind the fact that we are baptized and have the gospel. What truly matters is that we serve the One who calls us with a pure heart and with all sincerity" (*Opera Calvinus*, 46:128).

Duty and Inability

Hopefully you will say, "What must I do then?" You must make profession of faith in the congregation of the Lord in which He has placed you in His providence. You may not become unfaithful to the baptism you have received as a child. You must embrace God's covenant in the way of repentance and faith. Acknowledge that baptism calls you to serve a triune God. "This is the way; walk ye in it" (Jer. 30:21).

There is no other option. To say, "I will not do it; I do not want to give up my freedom," or to say in sinful passivity, "I will wait until the Lord converts me," is not the solution. You are no longer free to do as you please. You are already a member of the congregation. By virtue of your birth to Christian parents, you already belong to God's church. You will never be able to erase this. Your baptized forehead will always accompany you. Would you then negate your baptism by not making profession of faith?

You must consider that not making profession of faith is also making profession of faith. It is the rejection of your baptism. It is identical to becoming an apostate. By not making profession of faith you are in fact saying, "I wish I had never been baptized. I would much rather have been born in a family in which my parents would not have had me baptized." You will then resemble Esau who, as a desecrater, despised his privileges.

God has set you apart in baptism. Already early in your life, He has stretched out His hands to you in mercy. You are already adorned with the insignia of Jesus. How will you conduct yourself in light of this? Being under His banner, will you do battle with sin, the devil, and the world; or will you renounce Him and become a deserter? Then you will once hear from His mouth, "But those mine enemies, which would not that I should reign over them, bring hither, and slay them before me" (Luke 19:27).

Do you wish to maintain the bond which God has established between you and the congregation by baptism, or do you wish to break it? Do you or do you not intend to take over the responsibility of your baptism from your parents? A decision must be made—in favor of the church or of the world; in favor of or against God and Christ.

Oh, that you would say with Ruth, "Entreat me not to leave thee, or to return from following after thee: for whither thou goest, I will go; and where thou lodgest, I will lodge: thy people shall be my people, and thy God my God" (Ruth 1:16).

You may not postpone your repentance. As long as you remain impenitent, you are in danger of losing your soul eternally. Is not postponement one of the devices of the devil? There is only one way open, the way upward. You must fall on your knees with this whole matter. The solution is only to be found in a heartfelt bowing before God, in a repentance with the heart, and in fleeing by faith as a guilty one to Jesus the Savior. "Strive to enter in at the strait gate" (Luke 13:24).

There is no better place than to be on your knees before God. All other solutions are deceitful. It must become an unbearable burden for you that you must repent and yet that you cannot repent.

> As long as I am told that I must go to God and that I am able to come, it is presumed either that I am indeed able, or that I have learned that some ability to do good has yet remained in me. I will then give credit to myself for what should be credited to the Lord. The creature will be exalted and God robbed of His honor.
>
> If, however, I am told on the other hand that I am not able to come to God and I am not told that I must come, I am left at ease in my separation from God, who is not my God, and to assume I am then not responsible for my rebellion.
>
> If we preach that sinners are not able to come and yet must come, then God's honor is secure and the sinner has been cornered. Man must be cornered in such a way that he must come to Christ and yet cannot come. He must be told that he must either come to Christ or else obtain his salvation from someone else, whereas salvation is not to be found by anyone else (Acts 4:12). This is the gospel vise grip to shut up men unto faith.
>
> And when a man has been cornered in such a way that he must and yet cannot come, only the way of faith remains open. To be shut up unto faith is to be driven unto faith. God is thereby declared to be the only Lord who can save, and the sinner is made willing to be saved by Him (Prof. Duncan's address to the General Synod of Scotland, May 21, 1844).

I hope that in such a manner you will be driven to the act of making profession of faith. Even if you cannot say, "I have believed; therefore have I spoken," do come forward to declare, "Lord, to whom shall we go? thou hast the words of eternal life" (John 6:68).

— 6 —
PROFESSION OF FAITH AND THE DOCTRINES OF SCRIPTURE

What Does the Bible say?
To make profession of faith is to profess the Christian faith. One must know what he professes. Profession of faith must be preceded by instruction regarding the Christian faith. The earliest documentation regarding this is to be found in Hebrews 6:1-2. Anyone desiring baptism had to be instructed regarding the fundamental truths of Christianity.

Hebrews 6 mentions four matters which belonged to baptismal instruction:

(1) *Repentance from dead works.* This pertains to repentance from sin. The sins of their former lives as Gentiles are referred to here as dead works, being the works of a spiritually dead person which culminate in eternal death. The baptismal candidates had to manifest a heartfelt sorrow regarding them.

(2) *Faith in God.* This refers to faith in God's message of salvation through Jesus Christ. It is referred to as faith in God, since it is a faith in the God who has fulfilled His promises and has sent Christ.

(3) *The resurrection of the dead.* Baptismal candidates needed to be instructed regarding both the fact and significance of Jesus' resurrection from the dead, whereby it has been declared with power that Jesus is the Son of God.

(4) *The eternal judgment.* Instead of the Gentile notion of immortality, the baptismal candidates had to be taught that a day of judgment is coming when God will judge all His creatures.

Confession of the Truth
From the very outset, the doctrines of Scripture have been of great significance for the Christian church. The apostle states in Hebrews 6 that it is his desire to provide those Christians who already had

been baptized with further insight into the doctrines of Scripture. Rather than remaining focused on the foundational principles of the truth, they should seek to attain a deeper and more comprehensive knowledge. And indeed, also after baptism, they would continue to receive instruction as is recorded in Acts 2:42, "And they continued stedfastly in the apostles' doctrine." In doing so, they complied with Jesus' commission, "Teaching them to observe all things whatsoever I have commanded you" (Matt. 28:19).

The apostles repeatedly exhorted the churches to persevere in the doctrines which they had taught them. Paul exclaims to Timothy, "O Timothy, keep that which is committed to thy trust!" (1 Tim. 6:20). One of the primary requisites of an office bearer is that he must be sound in the faith (or doctrine).

In the New Testament, the word doctrine is neither a dull nor superfluous word; on the contrary, it is a very significant word. Instruction in Christian doctrine was a priority for Calvin. He strenuously opposed the Romish notion of a "complicated faith." One would then confess his faith without understanding what the content of this faith was, for it was the church which would believe on behalf of the laymen. The Reformers strenuously opposed this. They focused much on believing with the heart, but not without giving due attention to the content of that faith being the truth which is after godliness.

Faith and knowledge are inseparably connected. There is no faith without true knowledge. Calvin frequently speaks of the knowledge of the "heavenly truth," which is so contrary to the vanity and mystery of vain philosophy. "Faith...is not content with an obscure and confused conception; but requires full and fixed certainty, such as men are wont to have from things experienced and proved" (*Institutes*, 3.2.15).

This shows that Calvin viewed faith as an experienced faith that rested in a certain knowledge of the things it believes. On the one hand, he did not define faith in terms of pure experience, and, on the other hand, he did not define it in terms of purely intellectual knowledge. We can still learn much from this; we must always seek to sail between those two rocks.

Therefore, instruction in the truth was always a priority in catechetical instruction, and the profession of faith which would follow this instruction would have to be in harmony with the revealed truth of God as it is in Christ. It was not possible to make profession of faith without having any knowledge of the faith. Profession of faith was therefore always preceded by catechetical instruction. Only after it had been verified that one had sufficient knowledge of the true doctrine was permission granted to make profession of faith. This was the common procedure in the churches of the Reformation; young people would make profession of their personal faith in harmony with the truth of the Christian faith and the confession of the church. Making profession of faith never was and never can be divorced from profession of the truths of the Christian faith.

When reading Calvin, it is evident that he was not merely interested in the profession of the faith of one's heart, but first and foremost, in a profession of *the* faith, the Christian faith. The baptized members of the church had to confess the faith of the church.

Calvin articulates the manner in which he wishes that both catechetical instruction and profession of faith would transpire in the church. At an early age, children would have to confess the Christian faith during public catechetical instruction. Calvin viewed the reciting of the twelve articles of faith and the answering of the questions by young catechumens already as a profession of faith, for the catechumen would articulate the faith of the church. This would then be followed by a personal profession of faith at the age of fifteen or sixteen. "A child of ten would present himself to the church to declare his confession of faith, would be examined in each article, and answer to each; if he were ignorant of anything or insufficiently understood it, he would be taught. Thus, while the church looks on as a witness, he would profess the one true and sincere faith, in which the believing folk with one mind worship the one God" (*Institutes*, 4.19.13).

Making profession of faith is also making profession of the truth. With Calvin, we can assert today that it is because of insufficient knowledge of the truth that heresies have had such influence in the church.

Calvin said that it is essential that children be led to profession of faith by way of instruction, "to preserve the people in purity of doctrine, so that evangelical instruction would not perish, but that its contents would earnestly be upheld and transmitted from hand to hand and from father to son" (*Institutes*, 4.19.13).

The Importance of Doctrine

If one were to remove the doctrinal contents of the Christian faith, he would be left with an empty shell. Everyone would then be at liberty to define faith as they please. One person understands the Christian faith to be one thing, and another entertains a different view. One then believes in his own manner and according to his own views.

Is not this the evil that surrounds us? Man has "come of age" and no longer wants God's Word and the confession of the Christian church to dictate to him what he ought to believe. He believes in a manner that suits him, defining his faith on his own terms. This is ultimately nothing less than will worship.

Our faith must rest upon the foundation of the doctrines of the Bible. Scripture therefore strongly emphasizes the doctrinal content of the Christian faith. Paul exhorts the congregation of Corinth to keep in memory the gospel as he has preached it unto them (1 Cor. 15:2). The apostles repeatedly preached the same truths regarding the baptisms of Jesus and John the Baptist; regarding Jesus' sojourn upon earth, His suffering and death, His resurrection, ascension, and session at the right hand of God; and regarding the outpouring of the Holy Ghost and Christ's return unto judgment. In the book of Acts, we repeatedly encounter this stereotypical preaching of the apostles. This constituted the content of the Christian faith.

In addition to this, one finds in the apostolic letters an enumeration of fundamental truths which Christians are mandated to believe. Consider, for example, 1 Corinthians 15:1-8 and Philippians 2:5-11.

Doctrine is a matter of great significance. The Form for the Administration of Baptism therefore asks of parents at baptism, "Whether you acknowledge the doctrine which is contained in the Old and New Testaments, and in the articles of the Christian faith, and which is taught here in this Christian church, to be the true and perfect (complete) doctrine of salvation?"

Furthermore, parents promise at the baptism of their children to have them "instructed and brought up in the aforesaid doctrine, or help or cause them to be instructed therein." The church of the Reformation taught that parents were obligated to give their children catechetical instruction as soon as they were old enough to receive it. The Convent of Wesel went so far as to stipulate that parents who refused to fulfill this obligation be subjected to ecclesiastical discipline. By virtue of the Christian instruction given, the family had to resemble a little church.

The Reformers therefore composed catechisms to assist parents, the school, and the church in this task. They wished to communicate how important it is that baptized children are taught sound doctrine. They gave much attention to both the knowledge and preservation of sound doctrine. The God-fearing ruler of the Palatinate, Frederick III, wrote in the preface of the well-known Heidelberg Catechism:

> Since the schools were floundering, the tender youth were neglected. Christian education did not provide consistent instruction. In addition to other evil consequences, the lack of sound instruction in true religion resulted in children being influenced by all manner of error and thus growing up in great ignorance. When we saw such great evils and considered that neither church nor state, and much less a family, can prosper, and also that there can be neither law nor order among the citizenry unless the untrained youth from its earliest years are brought to true godliness by way of sound religious instruction, we felt obligated to use every means to oppose this evil.
>
> For this reason, we commissioned our theologians to compose in the High German and Latin languages a catechism of the Christian faith, based on God's Word, so that from here on in we not only will be able to give better attention to the youth, but thereby also ministers and teachers have a certain and steadfast rule by which they can instruct the youth, so that in the future nobody shall learn things or matters which are not in agreement with God's Word.

The objective of the Reformers was to promote sound doctrine and to lead young people to a life of true godliness. Doctrinal instruction was therefore absolutely essential. The entire focus was upon molding young people to become members who confess the name of a Triune God and desire to live according to this confession.

How can anyone arrive at such a confession of faith unless he knows what the church of all ages believes and confesses? Instruction in the fundamental truths of Christianity is therefore a must.

Thus, indifference toward doctrine is a great danger, for thereby the key of knowledge is removed. One will then say, "Doctrine is not what matters, but the Lord." However, in the meantime, the door is opened to various unbiblical notions.

An aversion for the confessions of the church usually must be viewed in light of the fact that people want to have leeway to embrace their own unbiblical notions. They reject the doctrinal standards because their own views and opinions are thereby condemned.

Someone may hold to the opinion that experience and feeling are of the essence. However, he who elevates experience above the doctrines of Scripture will become enmeshed in all sorts of feelings and experiences which do not measure up to the standard of Scripture. Such tendencies are very prominent among the charismatic movement. Experience is more important than anything else. One is not a Christian until he has experienced something very special. However, a testing of these experiences by the standard of the doctrines of Scripture is lacking, resulting in all manner of unscriptural fanaticism and ecstatic experiences. Instead, our experience must pass the test of Scripture.

This danger also occasionally manifests itself, however, in the orthodox wing of the church. Experience then has the final word. The manner in which one experiences something is the touchstone of truth. A person will then say, "Such and such a person experienced it in this manner." Thus, the experience of a certain individual will be elevated above Scripture.

If human experience does not pass the test of Scripture and the confessions of the Christian church, however, both the veracity and purity of biblical doctrine will be lost. Christian doctrine must constitute the basis for public profession of faith. A person makes profession of the faith that was once delivered to the saints (Jude 3). We need not formulate a personal profession of faith, but rather make profession with the church of all ages of our catholic and undoubted Christian faith.

Doctrine is not an end in itself. To have only intellectual knowledge is insufficient. Doctrine must be experienced. The power of the doctrine must be known with the heart. The truth must not only be known and confessed, but it must also be believed and experienced. The Christian religion is ultimately a religion of the heart.

A person may have tremendous zeal to defend the orthodox truth without giving any thought whether he is a personal partaker of it. Such a person can speak at great length about the necessity of the new birth and the mighty work of conversion, and at the same time state without any concern that he is not a partaker of it. "I have personally never experienced it," he will say with the greatest ease, "but I know that this is the old and sound truth." Personal involvement with this truth is entirely lacking. Such a person only professes the truth and nothing more.

I fear that all too easily we make a separation between the mind and the heart. Ultimately, we cannot make a separation between mind and heart; they function interactively. How can we believe something with our hearts and then reject it with our minds?

You may say that you believe the truth that, due to sin, man is subject to all miseries, yea, to condemnation itself. However, if you can quietly live on with that knowledge, do you then really believe this truth?

You may also state that you believe the truth that salvation is only to be found in Christ. With great certainty and orthodoxy, you may confess the truth that outside of Christ, man can only look forward to sinking away forever into hellish perdition. However, if that does not move you to seek salvation in Christ for your soul, do you really believe it? Do you truly believe these truths as fervently as you pretend to do?

Zeal for the truth without having experienced it leads to fanaticism and a party spirit. It will then be said, "The Lord's temple, the Lord's temple are we."

It is also possible that faith is viewed as a rationalistic event. It will then be reduced to historical faith—a faith in which experience is absent. Believing that Christ has died for you will then be a matter of fact. We must be on guard against both dangers.

Furthermore, we must also distinguish between major and minor issues. There are matters regarding which believers can and may have a difference of opinion. These are matters which are not clearly articulated in God's Word—the so-called *adiaphora*.

It is very unbiblical indeed to condemn one another regarding all sorts of minor issues such as the length of the church service, the use of an older or newer version of the Psalter, the color of clothing, the use of transportation on Sunday, etc. You will then be majoring in the minors by elevating your own opinion and tradition as binding to the conscience.

Calvin was very supportive of distinguishing between major and minor issues. He rebuked John Knox for endangering the peace of the congregation by his liturgical tradition. He wrote to him: "In your liturgy I observe many childish elements. As for myself, I am quite flexible when it comes to the *adiaphora*—such as external formalities and customs. Therefore, I do not think it to be a good thing to follow the foolish stubbornness of those who refuse to desist from their own customs" (*Letter 393*).

It is wrong to risk the peace of the church for the sake of minor issues. According to the Belgic Confession, this is even a mark of the false church, of which it is said, "she ascribes more power and authority to herself and her ordinances than to the Word of God" (Art. 29).

The sound truth can also be lost by overemphasizing minor issues. Instead of the standard of God's Word, the standard of man and tradition will be used. J. C. Ryle's exhortation is therefore very much to the point:

> I wish to raise my voice in warning against the growing tendency to be dogmatic about matters which are not essential unto salvation, by taking a strong stand when the Bible is silent, condemning those whom God has not condemned—and to elevate unimportant and secondary issues to the level of primary truths and the more significant elements of the gospel (*Warning to the Churches*, p. 38).

The primary focus must be on that faith delivered to us by the Scriptures and summarized and echoed by our Reformed confessions. That faith must be taught, known, and confessed.

However, the church may not be satisfied with an intellectual assent to these truths. Wherever this does occur, Christianity will degenerate into dead orthodoxy. People will stand up for the old truth and agree with it, but will forget the truth that "the natural man receiveth not the things of the Spirit of God" (1 Cor. 2:14). Too much is then attributed to man's corrupt understanding, as if man's intellectual capacities have not been tainted by the fall.

By nature we are not at all inclined toward the truth. We are enemies of the truth! We cannot tolerate the truth which God reveals to us in the Scriptures—especially not that truth about our unwillingness to believe and to come to Jesus in order that we might have life.

Dead orthodoxy leads to coldness and indifference. There will then be zeal for the orthodox truth, but the most important thing, to be partakers of it ourselves, will be forgotten. What shall it profit us if we defend the truth that God works conversion in a sinner by the irresistible grace of the Holy Spirit, as long as we do not know ourselves that God can make us willing in the day of His power? What shall it profit us if, in a weighty and orthodox manner, we can speak about the sinner's absolute state of death, as long as we have never become experientially acquainted with the deadness of our heart and its absolute inability to repent?

What shall it profit us if we speak with great reverence about the powerful conversion of others as long as we do not know anything ourselves about the excellency of God's power in quickening and converting sinners? How will it benefit you if you can argue from passages of Scripture that in Jesus there is atonement only for the elect and no one else, if, due to your own unbelief, the wrath of God continues to abide on you and you do not know the sweet peace of Jesus' blood in your heart?

Do not think that you are better than others because of your orthodoxy and knowledge of the truth. Only when you know the power of God's truth in your heart do you possess something that others do not have.

The experience of the truth is a necessity. Albert N. Martin remarked "that every congregation, however soundly the Word may be preached there and however much spiritual life there may be, is only one generation removed from apostasy. This will happen when in a congregation a new generation emerges which no longer knows by experience what the power of Christ's blood and the operation of the Holy Spirit is."

How true are these words! The orthodox truth is indeed the foundation, but experience is the building which is erected upon it. The truth must touch, wound, and heal you. Luther therefore stated that it is not merely a matter of grasping the truth, but much more of being grasped by it. That which has been stated at your baptism must take hold of you: "We are conceived and born in sin, and therefore are children of wrath, insomuch that we cannot enter into the kingdom of God except we are born again."

The truth which the Bible communicates to you concerning yourself must fill you with fear, concern, and sorrow. What power the Word has to unmask us! How naked and guilty I will then stand before God! However, the truth of the gospel will then make and set you free. And indeed, the gospel speaks of a salvation which is by grace and to which nothing of man needs to be added. This gospel proclaims, "And let him that is athirst come. And whosoever will, let him take the water of life freely" (Rev. 22:17). It sets Christ before you as a willing, complete, and suitable Savior and proclaims that whoever looks unto a crucified Christ and believes in Him shall not perish but have eternal life.

If you will then be asked on the day of your public profession of faith, "But whom say ye that I am?," you will answer with Peter, "Thou art the Christ, the Son of the living God" (Matt. 16:16). Your profession of faith will then not merely be a profession of what you have *learned*, but a profession "of those things which are most surely believed among us" (Luke 1:1). If matters are as they should be, it will be a profession of the truth concerning Jesus Christ, the Messiah and Savior sent from God—a truth which you have personally embraced because for you it has become a *living truth*.

— 7 —
The Relationship Between Profession of Faith and Faith

Why the Need for Examination?
After having completed the confession of faith class, the moment has arrived for young people to make profession of faith in the midst of the congregation. Before this takes place, however, there must be an examination by and before the consistory regarding their knowledge of the Christian faith. I have sufficiently discussed the reason for this in the previous chapter. One must know what faith he is confessing. Without knowledge of the Christian faith, making profession of faith is like a building without a foundation.

Another compelling reason is that, upon making profession of faith, one acquires all the rights of full membership and gains admission to the Lord's Supper. The consistory must therefore be convinced prior to this whether those who are making profession of faith are able to examine themselves and are thus capable of a proper observance of the Lord's Supper.

No Examination as to Whether one Possesses Faith
The question before us is this: Must there not be an investigation as to whether one possess true faith? Are not young people called to make profession of *faith*? Is not therefore an investigation whether such faith is present more important than an examination regarding one's knowledge of the Christian faith? Is this not particularly true since making profession of faith in the Reformed tradition is intimately connected with the Lord's Supper, and includes the request to be admitted to the Lord's Supper?

There is another pressing question we must deal with. If the examination only pertains to doctrine and life and not to repentance toward God and faith in the Lord Jesus Christ, do you not thereby breed hypocrites? Young people will then be compelled by the church to make profession of faith without possessing true faith. They are earnestly invited to make profession of faith, but after that, it is almost as if they are told, "You will not partake of the Lord's Supper, will you?" In light of all this, would it not be necessary to ascertain whether young people do possess faith? Ought it not be mandatory that they give an account of their personal conversion?

Our Reformed forefathers never conducted such an investigation. Why not? In general terms, this question has been answered as follows:

(1) One will not find such an examination prescribed in Scripture. People are always judged by what they profess with their mouth. As long as this profession is not contradicted by one's walk, we may not render a judgment regarding the heart. In the Canons of Dort we read, "With respect to those who make an external profession of faith and live regular lives, we are bound, after the example of the apostle, to judge and speak of them in the most favorable manner. For the secret recesses of the heart are unknown to us" (Head 3/4, Art. 15).

(2) Man is not a judge of the heart. Office-bearers would then presume to be in God's stead and be inclined to think that they can render judgment about the secrets of the heart. The church could easily render an erroneous judgment, for regardless of what a person would declare before the consistory, it would nevertheless be true, "For what man knoweth the things of a man, save the spirit of man which is in him?" (1 Cor. 2:11).

(3) Many who are truly regenerate are unable to tell how they came to conversion. What Jesus says applies to them, "The wind bloweth where it listeth, and thou hearest the sound thereof, but canst not tell whence it cometh, and whither it goeth: so is every one that is born of the Spirit" (John 3:8). This is particularly true for those who have been drawn to the Lord from their youth and have been converted without dramatic changes.

The final conclusion of our Reformed forefathers has therefore always been the same: We need to observe the fruits in both life and doctrine. "By their fruits ye shall know them" (Matt. 7:16). Beyond this we neither may nor are able to go. The church cannot judge the inner man.

Thus, the consistory examination is neither an examination of the personal faith of individuals nor an evaluation of their conversion. It is an ecclesiastical examination regarding their knowledge of the Reformed faith.

The oversight of their walk is exercised via pastoral work and family visitation. This will consist, for example in young people receiving special visits to speak to them about their intention to make public profession of faith and to stress the necessity of a Christian walk of life.

Making public profession of faith does not merely involve acquiescence with the doctrines of the church, but one must also be willing to subject himself to Christian discipline and to live as a Christian. These are the matters regarding which the church must exercise her judgment. Life and doctrine are the areas concerning which the church must exercise discipline and oversight.

Furthermore, it also needs to be understood that making profession of faith does not mean that one professes to be converted. Making profession of faith is not bearing witness to your personal, saving faith. This view is promoted among revivalists and charismatic groups. There one comes forward during the public assembly, confessing to be converted and to be a believer.

Making profession of faith is not the giving of a public testimony that one is converted. It is not merely a declaration *that* you believe, but primarily *what* you believe. One confesses to believe the Christian faith that Jesus is the Christ, the Son of the living God. It is, however, not sufficient to confess this intellectually only; the heart must also be involved in it. One makes profession of the Reformed faith. One professes the biblical truth that Christ alone is the Way, the Truth, and the Life.

Thus, regarding the eunuch we do not read that he says, "I believe *in* Jesus, the Son of God." Rather, we read that he confessed, "I believe *that* Jesus is the Christ, the Son of God" (Acts 8:37).

To make profession of faith is to declare what one thinks of Jesus and not in the first place what one thinks of himself. Man and his repentance or faith is not the focal point in making profession of faith, but rather the truth concerning Christ. The eunuch confessed this with his whole heart. He expected salvation from Jesus alone. In light of that, one can obviously also say that he believed in Jesus.

Thus, making profession of faith is to profess with your whole heart, and especially to express verbally, that Jesus is the Christ, the Son of the living God.

This does not mean that the church must not speak about the necessity of personal repentance and faith in Jesus Christ. This, however, does not take place before the consistory. These issues will have been addressed by way of faithful catechetical instruction during the confession of faith class, as well as in private conversation. One must know what is necessary to partake of the Lord's Supper after having made profession of faith. One must be able to examine himself.

The church neither investigates the inner life of faith nor demands that one can give an account of one's conversion as a requisite for making public profession of faith in the midst of the congregation. The judgment of the heart does not belong to the church.

This was the great error of the well-known Jean de Labadie. His goal was to have a church of elect only, and he was of the opinion that he could judge the heart of others. He thought that he could determine who was converted and who not. This stirred up much unrest in the Netherlands near the end of the seventeenth century.

However, we do not know the heart; only the Lord does. We are neither able nor permitted to say, "You may," or "you may not" make profession of faith. The church may not say, "For you, we believe that it comes from the heart; but for the other, we do not believe it." This is a matter between God and the candidate for profession of faith.

It is precisely this, however, that makes it so difficult for some of you to make profession of faith. It would be much easier if the church would say, "You may make profession and faith, and you may not." You must make this decision before the countenance of God. As long as you neither live in sin nor espouse heretical views, the church remains silent. Perhaps this is precisely the church's intent, and also God's.

A Tension that Remains
Thus, the church does not judge the inner man. The consistory will not ask you whether you are converted. It is also not customary in

our circles, as is true in other Reformed churches, that a promise is elicited from the candidates for confession of faith that upon making public profession they will partake of the Lord's Supper. The only thing that takes place is an examination regarding the knowledge of the doctrines of Scripture.

All this appears to be rather simple. If you faithfully participate in the life of the church and have learned your catechism lessons well, you will pass this examination with flying colors. It appears that beyond this there are no obligations to be fulfilled.

If, however, such were to be your thinking, you are mistaken. What the church does do is communicate to you via the preaching, catechism instruction, and the pastorate that God demands a confession of the heart. There must be harmony between what you say with your mouth and what lives in your heart. God's covenant obligates the baptized person to make a profession of faith; however, this confession must be made with both the mouth and the heart. God will not be satisfied with less. The church may not demand anything less than that, and you yourself may not be at peace with anything less.

How do we resolve this? Must we assert that one must wait until he is converted? In some circles this is the prevailing opinion. Thus it happened in previous centuries that people would not make profession of faith until they were sixty or seventy years of age. In some areas this still occurs. Only a few make public profession of faith and the remainder of the congregation remain baptized members for life.

This is obviously not correct. There is no such thing as baptized members who are thirty or sixty years of age, for baptized members are members under age. Such individuals frequently wait for something special and look for fitness within themselves.

Can we resolve this by contending that one should only make a confession of the truth? This is obviously one of the components of making profession of faith, but it encompasses a great deal more. When making profession of faith you are expressing by your personal faith that you embrace what the church professes to believe. This encompasses more than being in agreement with the truth taught in the church.

To confess with the church of all ages that Jesus is the Christ, the Son of the living God, is not something one does in a cold, intellectual manner. It is a matter which involves the heart very much. It is not sufficient to be fully conversant with Christian doctrine; there must be a bond of vital union with Christ Himself. The powerful words of Calvin come to mind here: "First, we must understand that as long as Christ remains outside of us, and we are separated from him, all that he has done and suffered for the salvation of the human race remains useless and of no value for us. Therefore, to share with us what he has received from the Father, he had to become ours and to dwell within us" (*Institutes*, 3.1.1).

We may neither justify our unbelief nor approve of living an unconverted life without God. It is to be feared that such an attitude opens the door to remaining comfortably unconverted and yet being a member of the church. It removes the urgency of making confession with the *heart*. One will then no longer feel his deep need and will be satisfied and at peace with an orthodox confession.

The problem will also not be solved by completely disconnecting public profession of faith and the Lord's Supper. Obviously, making profession of faith and partaking of the Lord's Supper are not one and the same thing. The one is not an automatic extension of the other. Making profession of faith and partaking of the Lord's Supper are separated by the doctrine of self-examination.

Nevertheless, we may not unravel the connection between the two—something which has increased during the course of history. When the Reformed Church in the Netherlands increasingly became a national church, it was no longer possible to exercise careful oversight over the membership. Therefore, the men of the Dutch Second Reformation began to exercise more and more oversight over admission to the Lord's Supper. With great earnestness, people were called to examine themselves and it was strongly emphasized that the Lord's Supper had been instituted for true believers only.

This was emphasized even more strongly in the churches of the Secession, so that it became a normal occurrence that one would be a member of the church without ever partaking of the Lord's Supper. And we have become accustomed to this situation as well.

This, however, was not the original intent. The congregation would anticipate that young people, upon completion of catechetical instruction, would make profession of faith and would partake of the Lord's Supper, thus making profession of faith open the door to the table of the Lord. The Reformed churches of the Netherlands codified this in Article 61 of the Church Order of Dort: "None shall be admitted to the Lord's Supper except those who, according to the usage of the church to which they unite themselves, have made confession of religion, besides being reputed to be of a godly conversation, without which also those who come from other churches shall not be admitted."

Taking this into consideration, there are many who are saying, "We must go back to Calvin! The congregation must again become a communicant congregation!" Their view is that the threshold to the Lord's Supper has been raised far too high. This was different in the days of Calvin.

Considering that during Calvin's days young people already made profession of faith at the age of fifteen or sixteen and would almost always partake of the Lord's Supper, one could ask the question, "Is this then the way it ought to be?"

Yes, this was indeed how it was! It was Calvin's intent to lead baptized members by way of a Christian upbringing at home and catechetical instruction in the church to a true confession of faith. It should be noted that his intent was to lead them to a true profession of the faith of the church, so that they would be able to profess their faith in a tangible manner by partaking of the Lord's Supper. As far as Calvin was concerned, there was but one true faith: a faith that unites the heart to Christ and thereby to attain to the adoption of sons through Him.

Furthermore, it was not Calvin's intent to lower the threshold to the Lord's Supper by negating the necessity of repentance and faith. He is the author of the well-known and penetrating questions for self-examination in our form for the administration of the Lord's Supper. No, Calvin's doctrine of the Lord's Supper is not governed by automatism, but by the doctrine of repentance and faith—something entirely different than coming to the Lord's Supper merely on the basis of your public profession of faith, simply because you have a right to do so.

No one knew better than Calvin that only the Holy Spirit can work true faith, and that this true faith is not merely a superficial accepting of Jesus. "We would not benefit from hearing the gospel hundreds or thousands of times if God would not work in us with His Holy Spirit, opening our ears and writing the gospel upon our hearts" (*Opera Calvinus*, 46:63).

The young people who made profession of faith during Calvin's ministry were not all converted. They were not all motivated by an inward conviction. Calvin frequently bemoaned the fact that there were so many hypocrites in the church. He thought that out of ten there was only one who was united to Christ by a true faith. And yet, he adhered to his vision of the ideal.

With God's blessing, he endeavored to lead his young people to a true confession of faith. These baptized young people belonged to God. They had to be raised unto Him and be led to a believing embrace of their baptism. In this way, they could also become worthy partakers of the table of God's Son—that is, upon loathing themselves because of their sins and seeking their entire salvation in Christ.

To achieve this goal, Calvin continued to minister to them by the preaching of God's Word and the use of the key of discipline, even after their profession of faith. His expectation was from God's Spirit, who, according to God's promise, would be given to the seed of the church (Isa. 44:3).

Thus, Calvin was not able to resolve the tension between the duty to make profession of faith and the necessity to do so with the heart. We also are not capable of doing so, nor are we required to do so. By virtue of God's covenant, the baptized person must either reject or accept the demands of the covenant. That tension will remain.

How then must we proceed? Indeed, there are important, practical questions that need to be answered in this regard. At stake are the sanctity of God's covenant and the need to keep the sacraments from being desecrated. We also need to address the earnest questions of young people who continue to say, "How can I make profession of faith?" Only one solution remains: the way of prayer. "Unto GOD the Lord belong the issues from death" (Ps. 68:21). You must resolve this on your knees. The Lord has said, "Pray, and it shall be given unto you." What an excellent way! Young people, pursue this way and the outcome will be sure.

The Need for Guidance
Upon reaching maturity, the baptized person must make public profession of faith. First of all, there comes a time when he can no longer be comprehended in his parents. He then assumes personal responsibility. God's covenant, of which baptism is a sign and seal, must be embraced by heartfelt submission.

The next step is the Lord's Supper, which, however, may only be used by true believers, "for he that eateth and drinketh unworthily, eateth and drinketh damnation to himself, not discerning the Lord's body" (1 Cor. 11:29).

The baptized young person finds himself in this field of tension. One cannot make profession of faith casually, but not to make profession of faith is also unacceptable. One cannot attend the Lord's Supper as a mere matter of fact; however, to disconnect the Lord's Supper entirely from making profession of faith is also unacceptable. How many questions surface here!

To whom should the catechumen address these questions? You should certainly ask such questions during catechism class, and it ought to be the desire of the catechism teacher to address these questions. However, how rarely this happens in reality! You could also raise these questions at a youth group meeting—which indeed occurs.

However, what guidance does the church give in these matters? Is not this specifically the work of office bearers? It is their duty to answer the earnest questions of young people and to show them the way. What we lack is what is called in the Scottish churches an "inquiry and question meeting," during which a young person may lay before the minister the questions of his heart. Questions pertaining to partaking of the Lord's Supper are also addressed.

The fathers of Dort, however, were in favor of such meetings. At the Synod of Dort (1618-19), it was not only decided that no one may partake of the Lord's Supper without making profession of faith, but there was also a recognition of the spiritual problems with which people wrestle regarding these matters.

During the seventeenth session, on November 30, 1618, an extensive report was presented about the catechetical instruction of young people. The report stated that every effort must be made to ensure "that every one attain a clear and comprehensive knowledge of the Catechism." Then, if young people, upon reaching the age of discretion, wished to join themselves to the congregation, the following needed to take place: "Three or four weeks prior to the administration of the Lord's Supper, they who wish to join themselves to the congregation must be instructed diligently and repeatedly at a given location, so that they may become more fit and capable of giving an account of their faith."

This advice of Synod is in essence a plea for a separate confession of faith class. Thus, the minister or catechism teacher was obligated to devote three or four weeks to give intense catechetical instruction to the young people who desired to make profession of faith. And once more we observe the connection with the Lord's Supper in the words "three or four weeks prior to the administration of the Lord's Supper." However, we read more in this synodical report:

> The ministers must exercise caution that they will only request such to be instructed of whom they observe that there is some noticeable indication of fruit, and of whom they know that they are concerned about the salvation of their souls. Along with this, all whose identical condition would stir them up to speak freely with one another should be called to convene at a specific hour. Such gatherings should be opened and closed with prayers and holy exhortations.

The advice given here is of great significance. Synod here declares that the ministers shall conduct special meetings with young people who wish to make profession of faith, and with others who are concerned about their salvation.

From records of the preceding sessions, it can be concluded that this was especially recommended by the foreign delegates. The English theologians were already acquainted with this in their churches and advised Synod that two types of catechism instruction be given. In addition to the normal catechism instruction, they advised that special meetings be convened for them who were preparing themselves to partake of the Lord's Supper "to gather in a friendly and congenial setting in order to converse with such individuals specifically about matters pertaining to the faith."

Several important issues come to the foreground in this synodical report:

(1) The minister must not invite all young people to attend these special meetings. He must exercise caution and stimulate those young people to make profession of faith who are concerned about the salvation of their souls. Indifferent and ungodly young people may not make profession of faith. They must be admonished regarding their indifference.

(2) Also, members from the congregation who are concerned about the salvation of their souls should be invited to attend, in order for mutual conversation to be stimulated.

(3) These meetings should be held during a period of three or four weeks preceding the administration of the Lord's Supper.

It is very evident that the objective was that these meetings should be prepared with great care. Christians who had attained to much assurance and liberty in believing had to be more or less dissuaded from attending these meetings.

Those attending the meetings would have to be in comparable circumstances; that is, a common concern about the salvation of their souls. If these stipulations were to be observed, it would foster conversation between such concerned souls among themselves and with the minister. The entire focus was that young people and other visitors would feel free to come forward with their questions and concerns.

Synod anticipated that such meetings would bear much fruit: "Within a short period of time and as a result of God's provision, the abundant fruits of this labor, both as to progress in the life of faith and in holiness of life, shall be evident to everyone and shall bring both blessing and growth to our churches—all to the honor of God, and the propagation of the Christian faith."

How wonderful it would be if in some manner this ruling of the 1618-19 Synod of Dort would be carried out in an appropriate manner! We must speak with our young people about the questions pertaining to baptism, profession of faith, and the Lord's Supper.

Conventicles (gatherings of the saints) have disappeared. Many young people have never yet heard from the mouth of a true believer who God desires to be in Christ for a guilty sinner. They also rarely or never hear anything about the wrestlings, the misunderstandings, and spiritual strife of God's children regarding the Lord's Supper. What a blessed effect would such a gathering, conducted by office-bearers, have! Questions could then be raised and be answered from the practical reality of the life of faith!

Thus, our forefathers were men who exercised care (also ecclesiastically) toward the youth of the congregation, and endeavored to give guidance and assistance to those who were concerned about their soul.

Making Profession of Faith Should be a Must and a Desire

There are no tailor-made solutions which would result in the coalescence of faith and profession of faith. We have concluded, however, that baptism calls us to make a personal profession of faith. And that must be our starting point.

The Lord caused you to be baptized. He brought you within the boundaries of the covenant. At that time, your parents made a profession of faith on your behalf, and, upon coming of age, you are now called to assume personal responsibility for this profession.

From your baptism proceeds an earnest call to repentance and faith! What a rich offer of Christ and His grace is visibly unveiled to you! Baptism proclaims: "As surely as the filth of the body is purged away by water, so surely does the blood of Jesus Christ wash and cleanse from all sins."

However, baptism at the same time pronounces a dreadful judgment upon all who despise the grace of God. It proclaims that it will be more tolerable for the cities of Tyre and Sidon in the day of judgment than for those who have despised their baptism.

You are therefore obligated to make profession of faith. Must you then not wait until you are converted, or at least until you truly feel your sins and begin to seek after Christ? I fear that if you wait until you are fit for it, such a time will never come. If you are waiting for something special, when shall this arrive?

Although we must maintain that this profession is a profession

The Relationship Between Profession of Faith and Faith 59

of *faith*, we must nevertheless refrain from rendering judgment about someone's heart. We would then easily lapse into Labadism and entertain the notion that by way of our requirements we can determine *who* may make profession of faith, and *when*.

You may not withdraw yourself by looking for all sorts of pious and ungodly excuses for not making profession of faith. On the contrary, if you cannot divorce yourself from the truth of God's Word, you must make profession of faith. Rather than postponing it, you must begin to make a prayerful effort to come to an understanding of the faith in which you were born and baptized. Seek to be instructed regarding the doctrines of God's Word by attending the confession of faith class. Prayerfully read your Bible and a good book. Go to the Lord with all the questions of your heart and also communicate them to your catechism teacher. Speak about these matters with people who fear the Lord. They will not turn you away. However, whatever you may do, do not withdraw yourself!

The way of least resistance is to escape from your obligation to make profession of faith by way of pious or ungodly excuses. However, the way of least resistance is not always the correct way.

Perhaps you respond, "But I am neither converted nor do I have faith. My heart is still so sinful and the world is so attractive to me. There is so much in my life which is not right and I repeatedly commit the same old sins."

Can you say, however, "And yet, in spite of all this, I cannot divorce myself from God's truth. I neither can nor desire to reject my upbringing. I neither can nor desire to turn my back to God and my baptism. I know that I cannot die the way I was born and that only in Christ is there salvation to be found for me"?

Are you saying in spite of all your strife and uncertainty, "Lord, I believe Thy testimony regarding Thy judgment and my lost state. And I believe the message of Thy gospel in Christ. I cannot get out from under it. I nevertheless desire to live to Thy glory and to forsake the world. Therefore, Lord preserve me and do not let me go. Oh, that Thou wouldest guide and convert me"?

Is this your disposition? Then you may make profession of faith and you need not despair about God and His mercy—even if you must say, "But I miss true faith, peace with God, obedience to His will, glorying in Christ, and all the necessary things which a child of God possesses."

In the Canons of Dort (I, 16), I read regarding someone like you, Those who do not yet experience a lively faith in Christ, an assured confidence of soul, peace of conscience, an earnest endeavor after filial obedience, and glorying in God through Christ, efficaciously wrought in them, and do nevertheless persist in the use of the means which God hath appointed for working these graces in us, ought not to be alarmed at the mention of reprobation, nor to rank themselves among the reprobate, but diligently to persevere in the use of means, and with ardent desires devoutly and humbly to wait for a season of richer grace. Much less cause have they to be terrified by the doctrine of reprobation, who, though they seriously desire to be turned to God, to please Him only, and to be delivered from the body of death, cannot yet reach that measure of holiness and faith to which they aspire; since a merciful God has promised that He will not quench the smoking flax nor break the bruised reed.

Wait for a season of richer grace, and expect this to occur by using the means of grace. Take heed to this as unto a light that shines in a dark place, until the day dawn, and the day star arise in your hearts (2 Pet. 1:19). Young people, "This is the way; walk ye in it!" (Isa. 30:21).

Furthermore, consider that you need not have a perfect and assured faith to make profession of faith. You will not be asked whether you are free from all strife and doubt, for even the strongest faith is subject to assault. Satan always attacks that faith which seeks for salvation in Christ. To all appearances, the faith which moved the woman with the issue of blood to touch the hem of Jesus' garment was but timid and weak. However, it was faith! It established a connection between her and Jesus. Therefore, make profession of faith and say, "Lord, if I must perish, then I wish to perish at Thy feet and at Thy door."

Let me conclude this chapter by quoting a portion from a sermon of Rev. Bernardus Smytegelt, which confirms that making profession of faith may not be postponed, but also that it must be a heart profession:

Are there not some present who have not yet made profession of faith and who are already eighteen, twenty, twenty-two, and even older than that? What is your problem that, having attained to such an age already, you have yet not made profession of faith? Why have you not done so?

Do you say, "That is not my problem. My problem is that I am still too young. I do not wish to be obligated to the covenant at such an early age"? Oh, poor soul! Is it a burden to you to serve God? Consider that you have been incorporated into the covenant at a much earlier date, and do you now wish to sever yourself from it? God desires to be served from our youth. How would you dare to come to God when you are old? Have you not served the devil and the world long enough? Furthermore, perhaps you will never become old. God may remove you from this world at an early age....

Another person may say, "I am not worthy of being a partaker of the Lord's Supper." If you are saying this in truth and not merely as a pious repetition of sound words, keep courage. It may be the beginning of a work of grace....

Yet another one says, "Oh, I am not able to come to the Lord's Supper." Do you know what you are saying? You say, "I am not converted; I do not grieve about my sins; I have no faith in the Lord Jesus; and I have no love for God." Is that true? How will you then be able to appear before God? How will you then be able to die?

Another one says, "Pastor, I have made profession of faith. You are right; the matter is settled for me!" How did matters get settled for you? By espousing wrong views? You wanted to get married, or perhaps you were compelled to do this by either your parents or your friends. But what really motivated you? Did you do it to maintain a respectable external appearance? Did you really understand the essentials of religion? Were you really fit to make profession of faith? Did you understand what was at stake? Do you understand it now? (exposition of Lord's 28 of the Heidelberg Catechism)

— 8 —
PROFESSION OF FAITH BEFORE GOD AND HIS CHURCH

A Public Profession

The examination by the consistory, consisting of an investigation regarding knowledge of the Christian faith, does not constitute the act of profession of faith itself. Rather, this is made before the congregation. The entire Christian congregation must hear and witness this event to enable the church to recognize one as a brother or sister of the congregation.

The baptism of an adult can only take place after he has first publicly professed his faith. One who was baptized as a child, however, has not yet done this. Although he is already a member of the congregation by virtue of baptism, he cannot yet lay claim to the full rights of membership. This can only transpire by way of a personal profession of faith.

Such a profession must be made publicly rather than silently. The latter would be contrary to the nature of making profession. To make profession means that one desires to make a public statement that he is not ashamed of the gospel of Jesus Christ.

Jesus asked His disciples *publicly* what they thought of Him. John the Baptist also demanded a public confession of sin, and the apostles did likewise to those who desired to be baptized. Timothy made a good confession before many witnesses (1 Tim. 6:12).

In Utrecht, it was customary during the seventeenth century to make profession of faith in the consistory room in the presence of those members of the congregation who desired to be present. Upon having answered four questions, the young people were addressed and, after prayer and the benediction were pronounced upon them, they were dismissed.

This practice, however, should not be emulated. The congregation must have knowledge of this profession of faith. She must hear the confession and thereby recognize the candidates for profession of faith as belonging to God's church. For indeed, one makes profession of the faith *of the church*. Whoever professes his faith does not do so alone, but in communion with the church of all ages. He then begins to sing in a choir that has a lengthy pedigree—namely, the church of our Lord Jesus Christ. In the light of all these considerations, profession of faith is made before God and His church.

The Questions

It is noteworthy that the church of the Reformation did not compose a form for making public profession of faith. For fear of reintroducing Roman Catholic confirmation, it was the common practice to ask a few questions, followed by the pronouncement of the benediction—with or without the laying on of hands.

There was no synodical decision prescribing the contents of the questions. In North Holland, the following questions were used during the seventeenth century:

1. Do you have any difficulty with any aspect of the doctrine of our churches?
2. Are you resolved, and do you promise by God's grace, to adhere to this doctrine and the fellowship of our churches as long as you live?
3. Do you promise, in conjunction with a godly walk, to diligently give audience to God's Word and to partake of the Lord's Supper?
4. Do you also promise that you will willingly submit to the Christian government of the church, as well as the administration of Christian discipline, in the event that you would go astray?

In Rotterdam, a different practice was in vogue during the seventeenth century. After the preparatory sermon before the Lord's Supper, the catechism students were requested to arise and make public profession of their faith. They were addressed as follows:

"All who by virtue of their profession of faith have been received by the congregation as members, shall arise and thereby publicly declare that they,

1. hold the doctrine which is unto godliness, as it has been taught here from God's Word, to be the only true and complete doctrine of salvation;
2. reject wholeheartedly all heresies and errors which oppose sound doctrine;
3. sincerely promise, by the grace of God, to adhere steadfastly to this sound doctrine within the fellowship of the Reformed church, and to do so their entire life and until the very end;
4. will always conduct themselves in a Christian, peaceful, and honorable manner, as is becoming to members of Christ and His congregation;
5. shall willingly submit themselves to all Christian admonition, as well as the good order of the church."

It is evident that there was no uniformity regarding the questions which were posed to the candidates for profession of faith. However, the various questions in use were the same in essence.

The questions of Voetius have become the most well-known of them all, and gradually they were used everywhere. Even today, these questions are most commonly in use in our churches:

1. Do you acknowledge the doctrine of our church which you have learned, heard, and confessed, to be the true and complete doctrine of salvation, conforming with the sacred Scriptures?
2. Do you promise, by the grace of God, to continue steadfastly in the profession of this doctrine and to live and die in accordance therewith?
3. Do you promise at all times to conduct yourself conformably to this doctrine, faithfully, honorably, and beyond reproach, and to adorn your confession with good works?
4. Do you promise that you will submit to admonition, correction, and church discipline in the event (which God forbid) that you may become delinquent either in doctrine or in life?

Upon a further study of these questions, it becomes evident that the one making profession of faith is asked to acquiesce with the doctrines of Scripture, and that a walk of life is insisted upon which harmonizes with this profession. The entire focus is upon doctrine and walk of life. The churches of the Reformation did not wish to proceed further than this. Only God can render judgment regarding the heart.

This practice almost entirely concurs with what the National Synod of 1618-1619 expressed in Article 61 of the Church Order of Dort: "None shall be admitted to the Lord's Supper except those who, according to the usage of the church to which they unite themselves, have made confession of religion, besides being reputed to be of a godly conversation, without which also those who come from other churches shall not be admitted."

Although these questions only focus on doctrine and walk of life, yet they address another important matter. In the second question of Voetius we read, "Do you promise, by the grace of God, to continue steadfastly in the profession of this doctrine and to live and die in accordance therewith?"

We read in this question, "By the grace of God." This phrase is more than just an insertion. Rather, it is the very core or essence of the entire profession of faith. If you were to remove these words from this profession of faith, the entire profession of faith would be reduced to an empty shell. Indeed, then one's profession becomes pharisaic arrogance and pride, and a lie before God. If that phrase were missing in the confession questions, a minister would not have the courage to exhort you to make public profession of faith, and a catechism student would not have the courage to do so. Such is the importance of the phrase, "by the grace of God"!

It has been said that every profession of faith is the profession of a martyr. Martyrs who endured and survived persecution were adorned with the honorable title of *confessores*. Such a title was esteemed of greater value than a royal crown. Even though we presently are not in danger of persecution, we are also required to be steadfast and there will be times that we will be mocked. How will we be faithful to our profession and live in accordance with it, unless we receive the grace of God to do so? If you were required to make profession of faith solely based on good intentions or a presupposed salvation, it would be a worthless profession. When making profession of faith, we must cast our eyes upon God's grace and not upon our own strength or godliness. It is a manifestation of God's grace when it becomes the choice of your life rather to suffer affliction with God's people than to enjoy the pleasures of sin for a season. By nature we are blind toward the preciousness of the Lord's service. We have no desire to live and die with God's people. What a grace it is therefore when God draws you in your youth to cleave to Him and to fear Him!

However, we also need the grace of God to remain faithful to this profession. If the Lord Jesus had not upheld Peter, what would have become of Peter after his denial? How then could we promise to live and die in adherence to the profession of the doctrine of salvation without the help of God's grace? This would sooner be possible in death than in life. Life is so full of temptations, crosses, and trials. Oh, how impossible it will be to remain faithful, in our own strength, to our profession of the doctrine of salvation! Therefore, may the words "by the grace of God" be the anchor which you will cast out in the storms of life, as well as at the moment of death.

With this focus, making profession of faith becomes making profession of the doctrine of *salvation*, to which you desire to adhere both in life and death "by the grace of God." One makes profession of a *gracious* doctrine. It is a profession of a God who has revealed Himself in Jesus Christ as a God with whom there is forgiveness. The content of the doctrine which you profess is, "By grace ye are saved" (Eph. 2:8). Only because of this can profession of faith be made! If salvation were by works and we would have to make ourselves worthy or merit something, there would be no hope. Since it is by grace, however, no one can say, "I am too sinful or too unworthy." The law will silence you and render you worthy of death, but grace proclaims that Christ died in due time for the ungodly. This truth opens the door of grace widely and it may be proclaimed, "There is hope for the chief of sinners, because salvation is by grace."

May the words "by the grace of God" be precious to you—and become increasingly precious. Let your eye be focused on this phrase when you make profession of faith before God and His church.

In Voetius's days, the candidates for profession of faith, upon having answered his questions, would each receive a personal benediction. Voetius was accustomed to say after every answer of "yes," "May the God who has begun a good work by His grace, and who has brought you hitherto, confirm you in this and perfect it more and more until the day of Jesus Christ." This shows that one was hopeful, and believed in love, that these young people made profession of faith with their heart.

Public Profession of Faith

Easter Sunday is generally the day upon which public profession of faith is made in the midst of many congregations. The question arises why this usually occurs on Easter Sunday.

In the early Christian church, Easter evening was deemed the most suitable moment for the administration of baptism, since baptism signifies fellowship with the death and resurrection of Christ. As Jesus had left behind His burial cloths and had risen from the grave, likewise those to be baptized had to die to the world and arise with Christ unto a new life. Easter was symbolic of a new life. Both death and the night had passed away.

The catechumens would therefore convene in a separate baptism chapel during the evening before Easter—the night when the resurrection was commemorated. There, illuminated by a lamp, they would remove their old garments and would be immersed in a large baptismal basin, after which they would arise as "newborn babes" unto a new life. Thus they would come forward on Easter morning, dressed in new, white garments. Upon entering the church from the baptismal chapel, they would be greeted in the church sanctuary with the words, "The Lord is risen indeed!"

For this reason, public profession of faith is still commonly made on Easter Sunday, for, indeed, this profession marks a new beginning. When you were baptized, you were neither yet able to remove your old garments, personally confess your sins, nor express your desire to forsake the world and follow the Lord as a new man. You do this upon making profession of faith, having now come to the years of discretion.

This event confirms that the prayers of both the parents and the congregation have been answered. At the administration of baptism, the congregation had already prayed that this public profession of faith might take place: "That they *then* may acknowledge Thy fatherly goodness and mercy which Thou hast shown to them and us, and live in all righteousness under our only Teacher, King and High Priest, Jesus Christ; and manfully fight against and overcome sin, the devil and his whole dominion."

And now, there you stand as a baptized young woman or young man, confessing that you desire to fight the good fight of faith and to stretch forth your hands unto eternal life. You should think of this on the day you make public profession of faith. You should reflect on what is referred to in the form for the administration of baptism as "God's fatherly goodness and mercy."

God's goodness and mercy have brought you within the sphere of the covenant and the walls of His church. He gave you parents who trained you with the Word of God. He placed all those people on your way who have been used as means to guide you to the day of your public profession of faith. How wonderfully the Lord has kept you! Satan and the world have tugged at your heart, and you have frequently been led astray by your sinful heart. But God's fatherly goodness and mercy always kept you and would not let go of you.

On the day of your public profession of faith, you must acknowledge this. In fact, you ought to begin this day by reflecting on this. Think of what would have become of you if the good hand of God had not preserved you!

The service in which the public confirmation of members takes place is always special. It is a very meaningful service for the parents who may observe that their children voluntarily desire to be joined to God's church. They perceive God's care, as well as the fact that their prayers were answered. It is a joyous service for the pastor and the consistory who have bestowed official labors on these young people since their youth, and may now see fruits upon those labors. It is also a solemn service for the congregation which receives these new members into her midst.

Above all, however, it is an important service for the catechumens themselves. At that time the minister will ask you to arise to answer questions pertaining to public profession of faith. You will be asked to profess the faith of the church by answering affirmatively, promising at the same time, in reliance upon God's grace, to remain steadfast in your profession of the doctrines of salvation—and to live and die in accordance therewith. At such moments, you know you are in the presence of God.

Coram Deo

In the presence of God! *Coram Deo* means to have God's eye rest upon you. You must make public profession of faith while being conscious of that fact. It is certainly true that we are always in God's presence. God is always there and He is everywhere present—within as well as outside the confines of the church. God's eye is always upon man. You cannot avoid God, however much one may at times wish that this were possible. "Whither shall I go from thy spirit? or whither shall I flee from thy presence? If I ascend up into heaven, thou art there: if I make my bed in hell, behold, thou art there" (Ps. 139:7-8).

Nevertheless, the Lord is present in His church in a special manner. There He walks among the seven golden candlesticks and holds the seven stars in His right hand. During the service in which you make an affirmative profession by answering the questions presented to you, you are in the presence of God in a special manner. You make public profession of faith in the first place before God. He is the great Witness at the solemn moment when you respond affirmatively. He who is conscious of this cannot but utter a prayer when called upon to give an affirmative answer.

At that moment, you stand ready to profess your faith and to promise solemnly that you will fight the good fight. Ought not then a quiet prayer ascend to God, beseeching Him for strength and grace to be true to this commitment? At that moment, you are enlisting yourself as one of Christ's soldiers to fight under His banner against Satan, sin, and the world—and one day, in His strength, to be victorious.

Hopefully, while yet at home, you will have bowed your knees in prayer. However, when called upon to give your affirmative answer, a prayer will again ascend from your heart, "O God, give me strength and grace to profess Thy Name, so that my answer will not only be the language of my lips. Lord, take me by the hand and make

Thy strength perfect in my weakness, so that I may be a true disciple of Jesus Christ!"

Coram Deo. How important it then is that one be upright! With God's eye upon you, you must be genuine and transparent, to the bottom of your heart. All external show is then in vain. Any attempt to mislead is doomed to failure. In the presence of God, it is of no use to pretend. God knows everything about you; He knows you thoroughly; He knows you better than you do. Uprightness under these circumstances is an absolute prerequisite for making profession of faith. Young people, be upright before the countenance of God when you make public profession of faith.

No, you are neither required to be perfect, nor is it important that you be persuaded that you can do what God requires. He who makes profession of faith while confident of his own ability is neither truly upright nor acquainted with the evil recesses of his fallen heart. Instead, one ought to confess with the apostle Paul, "Not as though I had already attained, either were already perfect: but I follow after, if that I may apprehend that for which also I am apprehended of Christ Jesus" (Phil. 3:12).

There is only one sort of people with whom God can have no dealings. They are people who are satisfied with themselves—people who are of the opinion that they possess everything and that they are capable of being faithful in their own strength. However, the Lord has never yet turned away a poor and needy sinner who comes to Him.

Therefore, flee to the Lord with your poverty and inability, and let your confession be the confession of the father of the demoniac, made with tears, "Lord, I believe; help thou mine unbelief" (Mark 9:24).

Thus, one makes profession in the very first place "before God." However, this is followed by "and His congregation." This is the second matter emphasized before answering the questions presented to you. By your answer, you are declaring before the congregation that you wish to live and die in accordance with your profession of the truth. As Timothy made a good profession before many witnesses, so you make your profession in the midst of the congregation. Upon hearing your profession, the congregation will then receive you into her midst, exclaiming, "Welcome to the battle!"

To dwell in the presence of God's church is therefore not restrictive but encouraging. If even Paul was encouraged by seeing his brothers again (Acts 28:15), then you may also confess that you are strengthened by the fact that you are not alone in this battle. Your profession is made before God's church, and thus the entire congregation witnesses that you desire to fight the good fight of faith.

— 9 —
PROFESSION OF FAITH AND THE LORD'S SUPPER

Open Communion?
Baptized members may not be admitted to the Lord's Supper. Many churches are of a different opinion regarding this. They practice what is called *paedo-communion* (communion for children), which means that children may partake of the Lord's Supper. Such churches frequently also subscribe to what is called *open communion*. Whoever wishes to join the congregation in partaking of the Lord's Supper may do so. Neither church membership nor one's convictions are then an issue. The Lord's Supper is open to anyone.

The views of our Reformed fathers regarding the Lord's Supper were different, however. They maintained that only those who have made public profession of faith, whose life is void of offense, and who are capable of examining themselves may partake of the Lord's Supper. The Lord's Supper must be celebrated in a worthy manner. Children are not capable of proper self-examination. They must first be instructed regarding the doctrine of the Lord's Supper.

The Reformers were also not in favor of open communion, for then the Lord's Table could easily be defiled. It would then be possible that people would partake who elsewhere are subject to ecclesiastical discipline. It would also be possible that people with heretical views could partake of the Lord's Supper. How would the consistory be able to exercise oversight over the Lord's Supper and keep the Lord's Table pure? The Reformers insisted that careful oversight be exercised regarding the Lord's Table.

Desecration of the Lord's Table by unholy people had to be prevented. Calvin therefore implemented the use of the table token in 1560—a practice which is still in use in the Scottish churches. This token was a small metal coin, usually made of lead, which the elders would dispense to those members in their district with whose walk of life they were acquainted. These people had to show this token when they wished to partake of the Lord's Supper.

Calvin insisted on having a personal meeting with all who wished to partake of the Lord's Supper. In Strasbourg, he had replaced Roman Catholic confession with a personal meeting with every believer who requested to be admitted to the Lord's Supper. In a letter to Farel, he reminds him of how often he has stated it would be of little benefit to abolish confession if it was not replaced with a personal meeting.

Such a meeting with prospective participants of the Lord's Supper would have to be conducted by the elders "so that the ignorant, though insufficiently instructed, would receive more adequate religious instruction, and that they who were in need of specific exhortation would also receive it—and finally that those who were troubled by spiritual concerns could be comforted" (J. D. Benoit, *Calvin as Pastor*, p. 152).

Oversight over Life and Doctrine

Oversight regarding life and doctrine of communicants was deemed necessary, and prospective communicants needed to be instructed for whom the Lord's Supper is instituted.

This view of Calvin became embedded in Reformed churches. For a period of time, it was customary that members would be visited prior to the celebration of the Lord's Supper. They who either led offensive lives or were indifferent were exhorted to refrain from partaking of the Lord's Supper. Our practice of conducting annual family visitation is still a blessed remnant of this.

At the Convent of Wezel (1568), it was already determined regarding admission to the Lord's Supper that "they who wish to be admitted to the Lord's Supper must forward their names to the pastor eight days ahead of time. Immediately thereafter, one or more elders, depending on the size of the districts and the number of candidates, must be directed by the consistory to inquire carefully regarding their previous walk of life and to report to the consistory regarding this."

During the early stages of the Reformation, it occurred quite often that members were not admitted to the Lord's Table. One would then be refused admission either in regard to one's walk of life or due to great ignorance regarding a worthy partaking of the Lord's Supper. This prohibition to partake of the Lord's Table was intended to be medicinal rather than punitive. Calvin wrote: "If someone is prohibited to partake of the Lord's Supper, it does not mean that he will permanently be excluded" (*Calvin as Pastor*, p. 153).

Such was the manner in which discipline was implemented in regard to the Lord's Table. This was exercised first of all in regard to life and doctrine, but also in a personal meeting (instead of Roman Catholic confession) during which one would discuss *how* to partake worthily of the Lord's Supper.

The Reformers were of the opinion that in this they were following in the footsteps of the early church. The early Christians would convene prior to the Lord's Supper in almost identical fashion as the Jews did prior to the Passover.

The Jews would come together to partake of the meal of the Passover. However, prior to partaking of this meal, the history of their deliverance from Egyptian slavery would be recounted. Subsequently, they would eat the Passover lamb along with the bitter sauce and the unleavened bread, and drink wine. They would then speak about their deliverance from Egypt, prayers would be offered, and blessings would be pronounced.

During this meal, they would reminisce about the history of their forefathers and the roots of their existence as a Jewish people. It was by way of the blood of the Passover that God had delivered them from the angel of destruction and had set them free from their bitter oppression.

The Lord's Supper, as instituted by Jesus, was an extension of this. It was also a meal. He instituted it after He had observed the Old Testament Passover with His disciples. The essential difference with the Passover was, however, that Jesus had said, "Do this in remembrance of Me."

His atoning suffering and death had to be the focal point of this meal. Christians were indebted to this death for their eternal salvation, and that molded them together into a new people of God who had been delivered by God from the bondage of sin and Satan. Jesus Himself was the centerpiece of the meal.

Nevertheless, the link between the Lord's Supper and the Old Testament Passover was always maintained during the first centuries of the Christian church. The central thought that God had passed over Israel for the sake of the blood of the Passover lamb, resurfaces in the doctrine of the Lord's Supper.

This becomes evident, for example, in a Lord's Supper sermon by Melito, bishop of Sardis, preached in 170 A.D.

> He came from heaven to earth to suffer for man; He became man in the loins of a virgin from which He came forth as a man; He subjected Himself to suffering by a body which was capable of suffering, and eliminated suffering in the flesh, and since His divine nature was not capable of dying, He became in His flesh the death of death by which man perishes.
>
> For as a lamb and a sheep He was brought to the slaughter; He redeemed us from the slavery of the devil, as from the hand of Pharaoh, and sealed our souls with His own Spirit and our bodies with His own blood. It is He who covered death with the garment of humiliation, who wrapped the devil in the garment of His suffering as Moses did with Pharaoh. It is He who defeated the devil, as Moses defeated the lawless one in Egypt who committed injustice by stealing the children.

Within that context, Christians understood that the Lord's Supper was only intended for the people of God, redeemed by Christ, just as the Passover was only intended for redeemed Israel. Just as an uncircumcised person could not partake of the Passover, likewise unbelievers may not partake of the Lord's Supper.

Only baptized believers could partake of the Lord's Supper. The early Christians not only carefully guarded baptism but also the Lord's Supper. In the so-called *Instruction of the Twelve Apostles*, or the *Didache*, we read, "Let no one eat or drink of the Eucharist, except those who have been baptized in the Name of the Lord, for regarding its partaking the Lord has said, 'Give not that which is holy to the dogs.'"

Justin wrote around the year 150 A.D.: "This food is called the Eucharist and no one is permitted to partake of this except those who believe that our teachings are the truth, who are washed with the washing of regeneration and the remission of sins, and who live as Christ has instructed us" (*Apology*).

Jesus did not celebrate the Lord's Supper with everyone. He did so in the restricted circle of His disciples. What is written in 1 Corinthians 11 regarding self-examination and discerning the body of Christ clearly indicates that one must indeed be able to give an account of what he believes.

The New Testament uses verbs in connection with the Lord's Supper which indicate active involvement. We read of taking, eating, drinking, doing it in remembrance of Him, showing forth the death of the Lord, examining one's self, discerning the body of Christ, and persevering in the breaking of bread. These are activities which pertain to a select group of individuals—namely, true believers in Christ.

It was therefore customary in the early Christian church to admit to the Lord's Supper only those adults who had been baptized. Prior to the administration of the Lord's Supper, the bishop would say, "*Ita missa est,*" that is, "Be dismissed." All who were not baptized, all children who had not yet made public profession of faith, and all non-Christians had to leave the gathering. The Lord's Supper was celebrated exclusively with professing Christians.

Since one also must be of a spiritual disposition, the bishop would exclaim, "*Sursum Corda,*" that is, "Lift up your hearts!" The congregation would then respond, "*Habemus ad Dominum,*" that is, "We have lifted them to the Lord!" The administration of the Lord's Supper would then follow.

Thus we conclude that profession of faith and self-examination are connected with the Lord's Supper.

Profession of Faith, Self-examination, and the Lord's Supper
Upon having made profession of faith, the way to the Lord's Supper has now been opened ecclesiastically. Having demonstrated that you are sufficiently acquainted with the truths of Scripture, you are now deemed capable of examining yourself.

After having made profession of faith in the midst of the congregation, you have the full rights of membership. To this belongs the right to partake of the sacraments, and thus also admission to the Lord's Supper. Since antiquity, there has always been a very close relationship between making profession of faith and the Lord's Supper.

Above the Compendium, which was formulated by Herman Faukelius for catechumens who wish to make profession of faith, it is therefore written: "For those who seek admission to the Lord's Supper." As long as your life and doctrine are not at odds with God's Word, you have the right to partake of the Lord's Supper after having made public profession of faith. In fact, it is your duty to do so. You are obligated to partake of the Lord's Supper.

However, you may not partake of the Lord's Supper as an unbeliever. You must, prior to partaking of the Lord's Supper, first examine yourself whether you can partake of the Lord's Supper in a worthy manner. The issue is not whether you deem yourself worthy to sit at the Lord's Table, but whether you can partake of the Lord's Supper in a *worthy manner*. The apostle exclaims: "For he that eateth and drinketh unworthily, eateth and drinketh damnation to himself." Only by faith can you partake of the Lord's Supper in a worthy manner.

Without repentance and seeking salvation in Christ, you cannot properly partake of the Lord's Supper. Thus, you must examine yourself whether you are in the faith (2 Cor. 13:5).

Although there is a connection between baptism, profession of faith, and the Lord's Supper, it is not simply a matter of fact that every one who has made profession of faith also partakes of the Lord's Supper. The one is not the automatic consequence of the other.

Many claim that it is inconsistent to readily proceed with baptism and to make matters difficult for coming to the Lord's Table. They are both sacraments, are they not? There is a difference between these sacraments, however.

Baptism is a sacrament whereby God confirms His covenant and its promises to us and our children. The focus is not upon the faith of the parents or the children, but on God's covenant and its promises.

Partaking of the Lord's Supper, however, consists of the personal act of coming to the Lord's Table in order to commemorate there the death of Christ and to have our faith strengthened. Personal faith in Christ is indeed an issue here. Concerning baptism, it is not written that one must first examine himself—even though the use of this sacrament may also neither be form nor custom—but Scripture does state this expressly regarding the Lord's Supper.

Thus, the doctrine of self-examination is the link between profession of faith and the Lord's Supper. Everything can be in order ecclesiastically, but in our consciences we must deal with the discipline of God's Word which declares for whom the Lord's Supper has been instituted. The church may indeed admit you to the Lord's Table, but you cannot go to the Lord's Table merely on the basis of this ecclesiastical right.

Partaking of the Lord's Table is a matter between God and your heart. Matters must be in order between God and your soul. How does the Lord view all this? If it is well, this must be the great question that should occupy your mind. You cannot merely rely upon the good thoughts a minister or consistory may have concerning you. Though men may say that all is well with you and that you may partake of the Lord's Table, this does not mean that you have divine approval to do so. Do you have a wedding garment? Do you belong to them whom the Lord considers as worthy partakers of the table of His Son, Jesus Christ?

The Lord's Supper has been instituted for true believers only. Question 81 of the Heidelberg Catechism reads, "For whom is the Lord's Supper instituted?" The answer is not: "For all who have made profession of faith." Instead, the answer is:

> For those who are truly sorrowful for their sins, and yet trust that these are forgiven them for the sake of Christ; and that their remaining infirmities are covered by His passion and death; and who also earnestly desire to have their faith more and more strengthened, and their lives more holy; but hypocrites, and such as turn not to God with sincere hearts, eat and drink judgment to themselves.

This answer makes it clear that you cannot partake of the Lord's Supper merely on the basis of a profession of faith. You might possibly think, "I now have a right to come, and it is my obligation toward the Lord, and thus I will partake of the Lord's Supper." However, you are then bypassing a very significant matter: the matter of upright self-examination.

In order to partake of the Lord's Supper and to remember the suffering and death of Jesus, you must also know Jesus and have learned to seek your salvation in His atoning suffering and death.

How else can you, in a worthy manner, remember the love of Christ who allowed His body to be broken and His blood to be shed for the remission of your sins?

In spite of the fact that you have made profession of faith and the door to the Lord's Supper has been opened for you ecclesiastically, you thereby neither have a divine right to partake of the Lord's Supper nor will it yield peace and freedom in your conscience to do so.

You are subject to the discipline of God's Word. That Word teaches you who are invited to come to the Lord's Table. Even though you have an ecclesiastical right by virtue of your profession, you need a divine right to partake of the Lord's Table. Therefore, after profession of faith has been made, the church is not a passive observer regarding participation in the Lord's Supper. The keys of God's kingdom have been entrusted to the church; thus, the preaching of the Word identifies those who are the worthy partakers of the Table of Jesus Christ.

We read of this in Article 35 of the Belgic Confession: "We believe and confess that our Savior Jesus Christ did ordain and institute the sacrament of the Holy Supper, to nourish and support those whom He hath already regenerated and incorporated into His family, which is His Church."

Then follows a description who these elect are: "Now those who are regenerated have in them a twofold life, the one corporal and temporal, which they have from the first birth, and is common to all men; the other spiritual and heavenly, which is given them in their second birth, which is effected by the word of the gospel, in the communion of the body of Christ; and this life is not common, but is peculiar to God's elect."

The question therefore is whether you have spiritual life. You have made profession of faith and you are permitted to partake of the Lord's Table. However, the question is: "Do I also have a divine right?" Do you have this two-fold life of which Article 35 of the Belgic Confession speaks?

Granted, every member ought to partake of the Lord's Supper. There are those who attend with ease, but there are also those who refrain with ease. And yet, there is not an automatic link between the baptismal font and the Lord's Table. Between the two are written the words of the apostle, "But let a man examine himself, and so let him eat of that bread, and drink of that cup. For he that eateth and drinketh unworthily, eateth and drinketh damnation to himself, not discerning the Lord's body" (1 Cor. 11:28-29).

One might posit that the apostle's admonition pertains to the offensive conduct during the celebration of the Lord's Supper in the Corinthian church and not so much to the disposition of one's heart. Granted, the apostle first of all has the negative circumstances in Corinth in view, where some would even be drunk while partaking of the Lord's Supper. During the preceding love feasts, some had eaten and drunk so much that they would partake of the Lord's Supper in an offensive manner.

Yet, there is a deeper meaning couched in the words of the apostle. Paul is most certainly concerned about the heart of those who partake of the Lord's Supper. Calvin comments:

> Some restrict it to the Corinthians, and the abuse that had crept in among them, but I am of opinion that Paul here, according to his usual manner, passed on from the particular case to a general statement, or from one instance to an entire class. There was one fault that prevailed among the Corinthians. He takes occasion from this to speak of every kind of faulty administration or reception of the Supper (*Commentary* on 1 Cor. 11:27).

According to Calvin, there are several degrees of partaking of the Lord's Supper unworthily: "Hence there are various degrees of this unworthiness, so to speak; and some offend more grievously, others less so.... Another, perhaps, will come forward, who is not addicted to any open or flagrant vice, but at the same time not so prepared in heart as became him. As this carelessness or negligence is a sign of irreverence, it is also deserving of punishment from God."[1]

Thus, 1 Corinthians 11 does most certainly address how one partakes of the Lord's Supper and with what disposition of heart. The issue is not whether one outwardly partakes of the Lord's Supper in a reverent manner, but whether one does so with a repentant and believing heart. The marginal notes of the Dutch *Statenvertaling* say: "That is, examine your heart and conscience whether you perceive a genuine sorrow over your sins, as well as a steadfast faith and confidence in the merits of Jesus Christ; and furthermore, whether you have an unfeigned intent to die more and more to sin and to walk in a new and godly life before God."

Everyone must therefore examine himself before he partakes of the Lord's Supper. The Form for the Administration of the Lord's Supper teaches us of what this self-examination consists.

The First Criterion for Self-Examination
The form for the Lord's Supper states: "The true examination of ourselves consists of these three parts." Thus, the form teaches that the doctrine of self-examination consists of three components, namely, the well-known trio of the Reformation: misery, deliverance, and gratitude. You will find this trio in all the writings of the Reformers.

The first thing concerning which we are to examine ourselves is:

First. That every one consider by himself, his sins and the curse due to him for them, to the end that he may abhor and humble himself before God, considering that the wrath of God against sin is so great that (rather than it should go unpunished) He hath punished the same in His beloved Son Jesus Christ with the bitter and shameful death of the cross.

Our partaking of the Lord's Supper involves a consideration of our "sins and the curse due for them." By nature, we have an aversion for this. We are inclined to cover our sins rather than bring them back to our memory. We have buried our sins and have, as it were, posted a sign which reads, "Digging forbidden." The consideration of our sins and the curse due to them is an activity we avoid. We would rather reflect upon our good deeds and qualities, and thereafter go to the Lord's Table with our good works, earnestness, orthodoxy, and zeal. However, in order to partake of the Lord's Table in a worthy manner, we must learn to consider our sins and the curse due to them.

We are inclined to avoid this self-knowledge and self-examination. It is the Holy Spirit who, in true conversion, leads us to consider our sins and the curse due to them. Just as the prodigal son needed to come to himself and consider how he had behaved himself toward his father, likewise we need to come to ourselves by the powerful convicting work of the Holy Spirit. Without such conviction, there will be neither true sorrow nor repentance toward God.

David's sorrow did not precede Nathan's visit, but rather followed it. We read of Ephraim, "Surely after that I was turned, I repented" (Jer. 31:19). It is the simple teaching of the Bible that no one has ever repented toward God with sorrow over his sin, unless the Holy Spirit first brought him face to face with the evil and sinfulness of his ways.

"And the curse due to them," is the language of the form for the Lord's Supper. A very strong word is used deliberately to point out that our sins are worthy of punishment. Our sins make us worthy of the curse, for God has said, "Cursed is every one that continueth not in all things which are written in the book of the law to do them" (Gal. 3:10).

When one knows his sins, he sees and feels that this curse rests upon him. Indeed, the matters addressed by the form for the Lord's Supper are very heart-searching. One must acknowledge that he is accursed of God. In that frame he must come to the Lord's Supper—not as a pious person, but as an accursed sinner, who seeks his salvation in Christ.

"To the end that he may abhor and humble himself before God": This is the fruit of a saving conviction of one's sin and being accursed of God. The knowledge of sin in the natural man leads to self-pity. He then blames others and circumstances for his misery. He who has truly been convicted of his sin, however, will abhor himself before God. Then he will no longer maintain himself, but will side with God in condemning himself. This will make him bow low and render him guilty before God. With heartfelt sorrow, there will be a confession of having sinned against Him. How good it is to be in the valley of humiliation and repentance! The deeper man descends into the valley of humiliation and becomes less in his own estimation, the closer he comes to God.

Listen to what the Lord says: "For thus saith the high and lofty One that inhabiteth eternity, whose name is Holy; I dwell in the high and holy place, with him also that is of a contrite and humble spirit, to revive the spirit of the humble, and to revive the heart of the contrite ones" (Isa. 57:15). This tells us that there is no more blessed place on earth than to lie, as a broken and contrite sinner, at the feet of a gracious God and a merciful Savior.

The form continues: "considering that the wrath of God against sin is so great that (rather than it should go unpunished) He hath punished the same in His beloved Son Jesus Christ with the bitter and shameful death of the cross."

By nature, we do not know what sin is. Sin is such a dizzying abyss that you would be utterly crushed if you were to look into it. There has only been *one* who has truly plumbed the depths of sin and who knows the measure of God's wrath which burns against sin, and that is Christ!

In His vicarious and bitter suffering and dying, His crawling in the Garden, and His desertion on the cross, Jesus has experienced how fearfully God is provoked to wrath by sin. God's wrath toward sin was so great that when God saw the sins of His elect upon His Son, He "punished the same in His beloved Son Jesus Christ with the bitter and shameful death of the cross."

The form for the Lord's Supper points this out to impress the evil of sin all the more deeply upon us. Its goal is that all who partake of the Lord's Supper shall know how dreadful the evil of sin is. The cross of Christ shows us how God judges sin. Sin merits death —eternal death!

He who confesses this may partake of the Lord's Supper. In this frame, one can commemorate the love of Christ who subjected Himself unto death for accursed sinners.

The Second Criterion for Self-Examination

Secondly, that every one examine his own heart whether he doth believe this faithful promise of God that all his sins are forgiven him only for the sake of the passion and death of Jesus Christ, and that the perfect righteousness of Christ is imputed and freely given him as his own, yea, so perfectly, as if he had satisfied in his own person for all his sins and fulfilled all righteousness.

This second aspect of self-examination pertains to the doctrine of redemption. In order to partake worthily of the Lord's Supper, one must not only have knowledge of his sins and the curse due to him for them, but also of the redemption and atonement which Christ has merited. The worthy partaker of the Lord's Supper must be a believer, for the Lord's Supper is a spiritual meal. Faith is the mouth whereby one eats and drinks Christ; that is, it is the means whereby one most intimately appropriates the atoning passion and death of Christ.

Without faith, one cannot receive Christ. To partake of the Lord's Supper without faith is no more than receiving a piece of bread and a sip of wine. Such a person is not capable of receiving Christ. It is the intent of the form that one would examine his heart whether he possesses true faith—and indeed, there is sufficient reason to examine one's heart.

Much faith is not true faith. There is historical faith which acquiesces to the truth without the heart being involved. There is also temporary faith. One who has such faith will for a season follow Jesus with much enthusiasm, but as soon as trials come his way, he, being disillusioned, bids Jesus farewell. There is also miraculous faith, by which one does and believes in wondrous things, without, however, his heart being united to Jesus.

A person is united with Christ only by true faith. Only of true faith can it be said, "Unto you therefore which believe, he is precious" (1 Pet. 2:7). Counterfeit faith does not involve the heart. One must therefore examine his *heart* whether he believes the faithful promise of God. Faith must be the exercise of our heart.

In what manner, then, must one examine his heart? As follows: "...whether he doth believe this faithful promise of God that all his sins are forgiven him only for the sake of the passion and death of Jesus Christ." When reading these words, we could draw the wrong conclusion that the Lord's Supper is only for assured believers, and we should therefore read carefully what it says.

The issue is not whether a person has an assured faith, and thus believes without any doubt, but whether he believes *the faithful promise of God*. The certainty referred to here is not to be found in us, but rather, in God's promise. We must believe that the promise of God is certain and truthful.

Faith rests upon the promises of God. Without such a resting upon the promises of God, there can be no faith. Calvin says:

> Free promise we make the foundation of faith, because in it faith properly consists. For though it holds that God is always

true...yet it properly begins with promise, continues with it, and ends with it.... Therefore, if we would not have faith to waver and tremble, we must support it with the promise of salvation, which is offered by the Lord spontaneously and freely, from a regard to our misery rather than our worth. Hence the Apostle bears this testimony to the Gospel, that it is the word of faith (Rom. 10:8).... Therefore, when we say, that faith must rest on a free promise, we deny not that believers accept and embrace the word of God in all its parts, but we point to the promise of mercy as its special object" (*Institutes*, 3.2.29).

By directing us to the promise of the gospel as the foundation of faith, we are drawn away from ourselves and are led to Christ. Hereby the foundation for salvation is not laid in us, but outside of ourselves in the atoning passion and death of Christ.

The contrite sinner who reflects upon his sins and the curse due to them is not cast upon himself in order to find something within himself. Rather, one is cast upon God's gracious promise of forgiveness through Jesus Christ.

What warrant is there that God will receive me in grace? Does one find this warrant in his contrition or hungering and thirsting after the righteousness of Christ? No; rather, this warrant is to be found in the promise of the gospel. We may flee to Christ with our sins and the curse due to them, since the promise of the gospel says that whoever looks to Christ the Crucified One, and believes in Him, shall not perish but have eternal life.

Without a genuine knowledge and heartfelt sense of our sins and the curse due to them, no one shall seek Christ and be desirous to serve Him. However, our knowledge of sin, contrition, and a desire for reconciliation is not the *foundation* of our faith. The *foundation* of our faith is God's gracious promise that whoever believes in Christ shall not perish but have eternal life.

In the gospel, Christ proclaims, "Come unto me, all ye that labor and are heavy laden, and I will give you rest." In response to the call of Jesus in the gospel, the laboring and heavy-laden sinner comes.

Thus, the distinguishing feature of genuine faith is that it trusts in the faithful promise of God. This faith is therefore so certain of its case that the form continues by stating, "and that the perfect righteousness of Christ is imputed and freely given him as his own, yea, so perfectly, as if he had satisfied in his own person for all his sins and fulfilled all righteousness."

Nevertheless, this truth elicits many questions. Few understand that there is assurance in every exercise of faith, and yet, this fully harmonizes with the definition of true, saving faith. Faith is therefore defined as such in our Heidelberg Catechism:

> True faith is not only a *certain* knowledge, whereby I hold for truth all that God has revealed to us in His word, but also an assured confidence, which the Holy Ghost works by the gospel, in my heart; that not only to others, but to me also, remission of sin, everlasting righteousness and salvation, are freely given by God, merely of grace, only for the sake of Christ's merits (Lord's Day 7, Q. 21).

The language of our form is not a foreign formulation. Yet, many will say, "I miss this faith as it is defined here. I miss the assurance that this is also for me."

First, we need to consider that true faith will be assaulted. We need not be jealous of those who look down upon the struggle of God's children. They deem such struggles to be unhealthy. They consider all this agonizing whether salvation is also for me to be superfluous. They are always able to believe and doubt is foreign to them. I fear that what Comrie writes is applicable to them: "O, my beloved, from the bottom of my heart I must say that I fear for many. They are haughty and speak presumptuously about the most advanced exercises of faith. They have never suffered pain nor anguish and are as little acquainted with broken bones as was Luther's prior, and yet they are masters at passing judgment on many" (*Exposition of Heidelberg Catechism*, p. 426). Therefore, I do not want to judge the strife of God's children in that manner.

Sometimes, however, God's children can entertain serious misconceptions. Instead of seeking the foundation for their freedom in God's promise, they seek it within themselves. Everything then revolves around whether a person has humbled himself sufficiently, whether he feels his sins enough, or whether he can feel that God is willing to be gracious and that Christ shall receive him. Rather than looking to the brazen serpent, he looks within himself.

Sometimes people look for very special things, such as a voice from heaven saying to them that God has loved them with an everlasting love and that Christ has died for them. One may have had the occasion to hear godly people speak about a revelation of Christ to their soul and then deems such a revelation to be of an extraordinary nature.

As far as God's children are concerned, there are many reasons why faith cannot break through. To be able to say by faith, "Not only to others, but also to me God, for Christ's sake, has graciously granted forgiveness of sins, eternal salvation, and righteousness," can be so far beyond their reach. Such spiritual misconceptions and ignorance frequently yield much doubt and fear, and Satan abuses this to keep many in a state of uncertainty—sometimes for years.

However, we also need to consider a different aspect. It is ultimately the work of the Holy Spirit to work faith and assurance. Only when the Lord Himself says to our soul, "I am thy salvation," can our heart be at rest. For the enjoyment of assurance, we remain dependent upon the Holy Spirit.

Even if we enjoy the benefit of healthy preaching and have interaction with biblical Christians, that, in and of itself, cannot yield assurance to our souls. The assaulted sinner can read the promises of the gospel in the Bible, a minister may proclaim them and set Christ before him in all His fullness and suitability—yes, even an angel from heaven could proclaim the promises of the gospel without the assaulted sinner experiencing their comfort and power.

The word of promise, however rich it may be, does not have the inherent power to accomplish this. The Holy Spirit must personally apply the promise. It is He who must convince the sinner that the promise is true and that it is *true for him!* Such is the manner in which faith is wrought in the heart.

The concerned sinner cannot simply believe the promise, but instead says, "I shall yet be excluded. It is for others, but not for me." But behold, the Holy Spirit assists the sinner in this struggle and persuades him that the promise is true *and that it is true for him*. It is as if the promise embraces the sinner and the sinner in return embraces the promise. Then he hears the message, "The Master is there and He calleth thee!" At such a moment, faith breaks through.

Though he earlier had to say, "It is for others and not for me," now he may say, "It is also for me—yes, even for such a one as I am!"

Then he will understand the question of the form for the administration of the Lord's Supper and will echo its words: "He doth believe this faithful promise of God that all his sins are forgiven him only for the sake of the passion and death of Jesus Christ, and that the perfect righteousness of Christ is imputed and freely given him as his own."

However, there is more in the second question for self-examination. It continues, "yea, so perfectly, as if he had satisfied in his own person for all his sins and fulfilled all righteousness."

These words could readily lead someone to conclude that he must possess an assured faith to partake of the Lord's Supper. If, however, such is your conclusion, you are not reading this correctly. It does not say that one must believe this with full assurance, but that Christ has made full satisfaction for sin. The issue here is the fullness of the satisfaction accomplished by Christ.

The only way you could know whether you had made full satisfaction would be if you had paid God the very last penny. However, Jesus has made such complete satisfaction! He has so fully made satisfaction for all the sins of His people that it is as if they themselves had made satisfaction. So completely has He taken their place before God and made atonement for their debt before Him! To this atonement, made by Christ, the faithful promise of the gospel bears witness—a promise which faith embraces. We must observe again that the focus here is upon the contents of the gospel promise.

This promise of the gospel, however, does not speak of a doubtful salvation, but rather, of a righteousness that is so all-encompassing, it is as if one personally had atoned for his sins. Faith embraces that promise.

Such faith is needed to partake of the Lord's Supper—a faith that, in the midst of a deep consciousness of need, clings to the faithful promise of God. It is a faith that knows of the blessed experience, "Now it is not only for others, but also for me!"

Let me conclude with the beautiful and instructive description Justus Vermeer gives of this embracing of God's faithful promise:

One needs to make a distinction between the promises of God in which all these great matters are comprehended, and the faith by which these sure and faithful promises are received and appropriated. We do not read that this faith must be an assured faith. These great and faithful promises of God encompass the believer's complete justification and pardon of all sins—all this solely for the sake of the passion and death of Jesus Christ. These promises pertain to nothing less than the imputation of Christ's perfect righteousness and obedience—a righteousness so perfect that it is as if believers have personally made atonement for all their sins and fulfilled all righteousness.

This is the essence of the matter of which everyone must be a partaker. Not to be a partaker of these faithful promises means that one will perish, and therefore the feeblest believer yearns to be a partaker of this great benefit. It is therefore of crucial importance that we have that faith by which God's faithful promises are embraced.

One can do this with a strong as well as with a weak faith; with much assurance, but also with much doubt; which much faith or with little faith. What matters is whether one's faith is genuine, and that, burdened by all his sins and wretchedness, one cannot live without Jesus; whether, as an ungodly one, one takes refuge to Him, thereby confessing that he would surely perish if there were no Jesus and that he seeks his life outside of himself in Christ, being convinced of the absolute necessity of being a partaker of Christ—and whether Christ has become precious to his soul (*Exposition of the Heidelberg Catechism*, p. 752).

The Third Criterion for Self-Examination

The third question reads as follows:

> That every one examine his own conscience, whether he purposeth henceforth to show true thankfulness to God in his whole life and to walk uprightly before Him; as also, whether he hath laid aside unfeignedly all enmity, hatred, and envy, and doth firmly resolve henceforward to walk in true love and peace with his neighbor.

The third aspect of self-examination pertains to sanctification. True faith purifies the heart. A faith that does not transform a man into a new creature is not of God.

The Roman Catholic Church accused the Reformers that their

doctrine of salvation by faith alone in Christ makes men ungodly and careless. Rome argued that if salvation is by grace alone, it does not matter how one lives. That accusation is unbiblical and false. The Reformers responded like the Heidelberg Catechism:

> *Question 64:* But doth not this doctrine make men careless and profane?
>
> *Answer:* By no means: for it is impossible that those, who are implanted into Christ by a true faith, should not bring forth fruits of thankfulness.

All who have become acquainted with God's forgiving grace through Christ's blood will tell you that their sorrow over sin and their desire to serve God have increased. John Wycliff, whose bones were exhumed and burned after his death, defended himself against this accusation by saying, "I have never lived such a holy life as since I embraced this doctrine that I am saved only through Christ and not by works."

Thus a person needs to examine himself whether he is inclined to live unto God. He must examine the inclination and sincerity of his heart. The requirement is not that a person must keep God's commandments perfectly, but whether he is inclined to live uprightly before God.

If you are a child of God, there can be much that will fill you with sorrow and shame. However, as to the inclination of your heart, you will dare to say with Peter, "Lord, Thou knowest all things. Thou knowest that I love Thee." In spite of the evil that cleaves to you, you will have a sincere desire to live unto God. You will be able to say wholeheartedly, "I wish that all sin in me were dead."

A regenerate person has a new inclination. Even if there were neither a heaven full of light nor a hell full of darkness, he would desire to serve God and to live before Him without sin.

Sin and Satan are the lord and master of the unregenerate heart. The power of sin has never been broken, even though it may be kept in check by a person's upbringing and conscience.

This is not the case with the regenerate person. His heart has been renewed; a new principle and inclination have been planted in his heart. Christ has ascended the throne of his heart. Sin is no longer lord and master.

Why then does a child of God still have so much struggle with sin? He will complain much more about his evil heart and the power of sin than prior to his conversion. Struggle with sin is a healthy sign. It proves that one is no longer a slave to sin. On the contrary, new desires and a new inclination have been planted in his heart. It is this new inclination which causes him to live uprightly before God. This renewal of the heart also yields a desire to live in love and peace with one's neighbor.

This concludes the self-examination required for partaking of the Lord's Supper. He who partakes of the Lord's Supper is indeed a sinner; however, he is a *renewed* sinner. The only proof that a person is in Christ, and He in him, is a sanctified walk of life. It is one's life that proves to which family he belongs. Therefore one may not glory in Christ's work *for* him unless he shows by his life that Christ is at work *in* him.

The Worthy Partaker of the Lord's Supper

After the third question for self-examination, the form for the Lord's Supper continues: "All those, then, who are thus disposed, God will certainly receive in mercy and count them worthy partakers of the table of His Son Jesus Christ."

How comforting and encouraging that is! If these questions for self-examination express what lives in your heart and you are thus inclined, God will receive you in grace. In God's sight, you are a worthy partaker of the table of His Son Jesus Christ. What an honor! It is almost too great to believe. Fallen sinners who acquiesce in their own condemnation are partakers of the table of God's Son!

This elicits questions in many concerned Christians. Perhaps you too have difficulty with the expression, "all those, then, who are thus disposed." Your question is, "Am I thus disposed?"

The touchstone for self-examination has been given in these three questions. The question, however, is, "Are the marks of worthy partakers of the Lord's Table found in me?" Let us listen to Brakel:

(1) A true believer will perceive within himself that with all his heart—albeit the one time more perceptibly than at other times—he yearns for the Lord Jesus in order to be justified by His blood, to be clothed with His holiness as merited by His ful-

fillment of the law, and to be renewed and sanctified by His Spirit. He will perceive that he yearns for, longs for, cries after, flees to, waits upon, and surrenders himself to Him. He wrestles against unbelief in order that he may bring Jesus into his heart, and to be assured that he believes in Him and is a partaker of Him and His benefits.

(2) He will perceive that he cannot be satisfied with believing that he has received grace. He desires with all his heart the possession, the enjoyment, and the relish of the benefits of the covenant. He will perceive that he is enamored with being truly united to God, with a life in which there is an impression of the Lord's presence, with peace of conscience, and with the love and fear of the Lord. When he misses this, he is troubled, and if he has lost this, he cannot rest until he receives it by renewal; for this is his life, delight, and felicity.

(3) He will perceive within himself a hatred and distaste for sin, a grief when he sins, a repeated rising again and a fleeing to the blood of Jesus unto reconciliation, and a delight and love to live a life which is pleasing to the Lord. He perceives within himself a warfare between the flesh and the spirit. The lusts of the world continually draw him to the world and away from God, whereas the spirit—that which has been regenerated, his spiritual life within him—continually draws him away from sin unto God. He also perceives, to his grief, that the flesh at times has the upper hand in this battle, whereas at other times, to his joy, the spirit prevails.

Such may not refrain from partaking, but rather are obligated to come forward with the multitude which keeps holyday, so that by using the signs, the promises—which are made to such as have just been mentioned—may be sealed to them (*The Christian's Reasonable Service*, Vol. 2, p. 581).

The form for the Lord's Supper itself continues in a very pastoral tone. The reading of the form, when blessed by the Lord, can resolve many difficulties. How pastorally we are addressed: "For we do not come to this supper to testify thereby that we are perfect and righteous in ourselves; but on the contrary, considering that we seek our life out of ourselves in Jesus Christ we acknowledge that we lie in the midst of death."

That is the basis upon which a guilty and condemned sinner

comes to the Lord's Supper. The grounds for coming are not within yourself—not even in your experiences, though they cannot be lacking as the evidence of faith. The foundation for coming is to be found in Christ's atoning passion and death. The true partaker of the Lord's Supper seeks his life outside of himself in Christ. The core truth regarding partaking of the Lord's Supper remains: "Whereas you should otherwise have suffered eternal death, I have given my body to the death of the cross and shed my blood for you." The eye of faith must be fixed upon that truth, and that truth must be remembered at the Lord's table.

What about one's worthiness? Let me conclude with the words of Calvin:

> How shall we, who are devoid of all good, polluted by the defilements of sin, and half dead, worthily eat the body of the Lord? We shall rather consider that we, who are poor, are coming to a benevolent giver, sick to a physician, sinful to the author of righteousness, in fine, dead to him who gives life; that worthiness which is commanded by God, consists especially in faith, which places all things in Christ, nothing in ourselves (*Institutes*, 4.17.42).

Calvin goes on to say that your unworthiness is your best worthiness. This sense of unworthiness, which is the fruit of acquaintance with God and self, must be there. For there is also another possibility. The form for the Lord's Supper states, "On the contrary, those who do not feel this testimony in their hearts, eat and drink judgment to themselves." Be upright in dealing with your soul! Consider that the first question of a contrite heart is, "What must I do to be saved?" It does not begin with the Lord's Supper.

A person does not come to the Lord's Supper to obtain faith. He must acquire faith by means of the preaching of the gospel and the operation of the Holy Ghost. I fear that at times the decision to partake of the Lord's Supper is made too early. One may possibly grieve over sin and be jealous of God's people, and yet have not learned at all to seek salvation outside of himself in the Lord Jesus. However, the latter is so essential for partaking of the Lord's Supper. Without having any knowledge of the Lord Jesus by faith, a person cannot fruitfully partake of the Lord's Supper. How can we remember someone we do not know?

Do not partake of the Lord's Supper for the sake of the Lord's Supper itself. When you arise and take your seat at the table, you must be able to say why you arose and came. You must be able to say, "Lord, Thou knowest that I seek Jesus which was crucified."

---

[1]This quote is taken from the Calvin Society Translation and differs slightly from the Dutch translation.

— 10 —
Profession of Faith and the Church

Why Make Profession of Faith?
By making profession of faith, a person becomes an adult member of the congregation. It is a conscious act of affiliation with the congregation. One could ask, "Why is this necessary? Why do I need to be a professing member of the church? Can I not be a Christian without being affiliated with a specific congregation?" One might also put it this way: "One Sunday I will worship here, and the next Sunday elsewhere. Is affiliation with the church that important? It is the most important thing, is it not, to be converted and to have true faith? The ultimate question will not be, 'To which church did you belong?'

"Furthermore, if I must be affiliated with a church, which church must that be? There are so many churches and denominations, each of which claim to possess the truth. Besides, is there such a thing as a pure church? Every church has its own deficiencies, does it not?"

A People in Pursuit of Salvation
In response to these questions, let me quote what our Belgic Confession, in harmony with God's Word, says concerning the church. In Article 28, we read,

> We believe, since this holy congregation is an assembly of those who are saved, and out of it there is no salvation, that no person of whatsoever state or condition he may be, ought to withdraw himself to live in a separate state from it; but that all men are in duty bound to join and unite themselves with it; maintaining the unity of the church; submitting themselves to the doctrine and discipline thereof; bowing their necks under the yoke of Jesus Christ; and as mutual members of the same body, serving to the edification of the brethren, according to the talents God has given them.

We observe immediately that the Reformers had a high view of the church. The church is not a club of like-minded people who are all on the same wavelength on various issues. Instead, the church "is an assembly of those who are saved." This appears to be a presumptive and exclusive point of view.

If one were to interpret this description of the church to mean that "only members from our church will be saved," and "we are the only true church," such a claim would indeed be presumptuous and partial. In former days such claims were made, and are still made today in some churches. When making such a claim, one is saying that the boundaries of God's kingdom run parallel with the boundaries of a given denomination.

This, however, is not what Article 28 of the Belgic Confession is saying, and this is certainly not the intent of the expression that the church "is an assembly of those who are saved." One must interpret this as a humble acknowledgment of God's grace. The early Christians called themselves "the people of God." This was not an expression of complacency and pride, but an acknowledgment of the grace which God had glorified in them. They once belonged to this present world, but now they may belong to the people who are in pursuit of eternal salvation.

In Acts 2:47, the church is described in similar language: "And the Lord added to the church daily such as should be saved." The original text actually states, "such as are in pursuit of salvation."

The Bible speaks in lofty terms about the church. That becomes evident when we take notice of the names attributed to the church. Scripture refers to the church as "the body of Christ." Jesus calls the church "His flock," consisting of sheep unto whom He would "give eternal life" (John 10:28). The church is the bride and congregation of Jesus, against which He has said that the gates of hell will not prevail. Scripture also refers to the church as the temple of God and the dwelling place of the Holy Ghost (Eph. 2:22; 1 Cor. 3:16).

How is it possible that Scripture can speak about the church in such lofty terms? Are not the most eminent believers tainted by sin, and can we be that sure that they will persevere and be saved?

Scripture uses such language because true believers are united with Christ their Head. Believers have been purchased by Jesus' blood, are kept by His power, and are filled with the gifts of God's Spirit. For this reason the church "is an assembly of those who are saved."

Not everything that denominates itself as church is the church. The Lord Jesus has said, "Upon this rock I will build my church" (Matt. 16:18). He builds His church upon the confession, "Thou art the Christ, the Son of the living God" (Matt. 16:16). Where that confession is absent, the church does not exist.

The church father Cyprian said, *"Ubi Christus ibi Ecclesia,"* that is, "Where Christ is, there is the church." Thus, wherever Christ is neither professed nor proclaimed, the church does not exist. However, wherever that confession is adhered to, there is the church. She may be small or unattractive, or she may have shortcomings and deficiencies, but when this confession is truly functional, Jesus will build His church there.

Though there may be hypocrites in the church, the true members of the church are united to Christ by faith. It is with these believers in mind that the apostle writes, "Unto the church of God which is at Corinth, to them that are sanctified in Christ Jesus, called to be saints, with all that in every place call upon the name of Jesus Christ our Lord, both theirs and ours" (1 Cor. 1:2). All those who by a true faith are united to Christ constitute the church, wherever they may assemble.

The church is a community founded by Christ. Christianity is more than a religion of individuals. It is a community of people "all expecting their salvation in Jesus Christ, being washed by His blood, sanctified and sealed by the Holy Ghost" (Belgic Confession, Art. 27).

This molds them into a unified organism, consisting of "one Lord, one faith, one baptism, one God and Father of all, who is above all, and through all, and in you all" (Eph. 4:5-6). A Christian is a member of a spiritual community that assembles itself in the name of Christ, and feels himself united to all who love the name of Jesus in sincerity.

Since this is the essence of the church, it can be said of her "that out of it there is no salvation." This expression was first used by Cyprian. After him, similar expressions about the Christian church are used by Augustine, as well as by Calvin who also wanted to maintain this presupposition. He writes, "Moreover, beyond the pale of the church no forgiveness of sins, no salvation, can be hoped for" (*Institutes*, 4.1.4).

It may seem that such a statement is of Roman Catholic origin. Our Reformers, however, at the risk of being misunderstood, made such claims for the Christian church.

He who desires to be saved must join himself to the people of God. He must forsake the fellowship of the world, which lies in darkness, and become a member of that assembly which is in pursuit of eternal salvation (Acts 2:47). He may not remain on the sidelines, but must affiliate with the people who are in pursuit of eternal redemption.

To Which Church Must I Join Myself?

With which church must I then affiliate myself? Many denominations claim to be the true church. The true church becomes visible in the sound preaching of the gospel, the proper administration of the sacraments, and the exercise of ecclesiastical discipline. These are the things you must look for. Your affiliation with a denomination must be the result of a prayerful searching of the Scriptures. Thus, we read in Article 29 of the Belgic Confession: "We believe that we ought diligently and circumspectly to discern from the Word of God which is the true church, since all sects which are in the world assume to themselves the name of the church."

Not much has changed since Guido De Brès wrote this article. Many sects and organizations refer to themselves as the true church. They claim, "The Lord's temple, the Lord's temple are we!"

People then seek to define their own denomination by denouncing other denominations and thereby promoting exclusivity. Such people will say, "You must join us. By us everything is still sound and the way things used to be. We still have the old truth!"

The Roman Catholic church and many others use the teaching of Article 28 of the Belgic Confession to plead the cause of their own denomination. They use the language of this article by saying, "'Out of it (the church) there is no salvation.' If, therefore, you desire to be saved, you must join with us." It is noteworthy that such people do not seek to bring others into union with Christ, but with themselves and their own views.

This compels us to search carefully. What is the touchstone to be used in examining a church community which refers to itself as the church of Christ? Our Belgic Confession again shows us the way. In Article 29, we read,

> The marks by which the true church is known are these: if the pure doctrine of the gospel is preached therein; if she maintains the pure administration of the sacraments as instituted by Christ; if church discipline is exercised in punishing of sin; in short, if all things are managed according to the pure Word of God, all things contrary thereto rejected, and Jesus Christ acknowledged as the only Head of the church.

These are the main issues by which one must judge a denomination. The Reformers refused to identify the true church with either a building, a name, or an organization. Wherever the Word of God is soundly preached and the sacraments are properly administered, that is the church of Christ. One must join himself to that church where nothing is either subtracted from or added to the Word of God.

Obviously there have always been hypocrites in the church, and the purest manifestation of the church has deficiencies. However, when the above three characteristics are functioning, one may not withdraw from her.

You also need to consider that God's providence has directed you to the church in which you were baptized. The Lord could also have directed matters in such a way that you would have been born as a Muslim or within the Roman Catholic church. Instead, He caused you to be born in a church where, in spite of all her deficiencies, God's Word is soundly preached, the sacraments are properly administered, and Christian discipline is exercised. This is not a small matter! A person is not at leisure to leave such a church. You must have very good reasons for doing so, for to separate yourself from a church in which God's Word is soundly preached is a great sin.

Calvin writes: "For such is the value which the Lord sets on the communion of his church, that all who contumaciously alienate themselves from any Christian society, in which the true ministry of his word and sacraments is maintained, he regards as deserters of religion.... Whence it follows, that revolt from the church is denial of God and Christ" (*Institutes*, 4.1.10). Only when the church teaches false doctrine may a person leave the church. You may neither leave the church nor precipitate a schism for secondary issues.

You also cannot excuse yourself from affiliation with the church by pointing to the many deficiencies to be observed in her members. The authenticity of the church is not contingent upon the weak faith and imperfect obedience of God's children. The true church is where the Word of Christ is present. There, the Lord gathers His church and dwells with His Spirit. You may not disassociate yourself from such a church. Calvin says,

> Let both points therefore, be regarded as fixed; first, there is no excuse for him who spontaneously abandons the external communion of a church in which the word of God is preached and the sacraments are administered; secondly, that notwithstanding of the faults of a few or of many, there is nothing to prevent us from there duly professing our faith in the ordinances instituted by God (*Institutes*, 4.1.19).

Thus, the true church becomes visible in sound doctrine and purity of worship, and everyone is duty bound to affiliate with this manifestation of Christ's church. All individualism must therefore be condemned. According to the New Testament, being a Christian consists in being a member of the Christian church. With the Apostles' Creed, we confess, "I believe in the communion of saints."

True Christians who seek their salvation in Christ will not remain isolated; they will form a community. You need to be affiliated with that church community, for she is the assembly of those that shall be saved.

You may not affiliate with the world, for that is the community of those who will perish eternally. Instead, you need to affiliate with those who fear God and seek their salvation in Christ. The narrow way leads to everlasting life.

You must therefore give heed to the marks of the visible church, for the true church becomes visible in preaching and worship. You must not affiliate with a false church in which you do not hear what Jesus and the apostles have preached, "Repent, and believe the gospel." There people are put to sleep by telling them, "Peace and safety" (1 Thess. 5:3).

You must be where nothing is held back in the preaching of the Word, where nothing is held back regarding the dreadful reality of sin and God's wrath, but also where nothing is held back regarding salvation in Christ, as well as the power and all-sufficiency of His blood.

Finally, you must consider that without regeneration no one will enter the Kingdom of Heaven. Even if you were to affiliate with the best church, only true union with Christ by faith will give entrance into the eternal Kingdom of God.

The Yoke of Christ

The church is the sheepfold in which Christ gathers, nourishes, and cares for His sheep. By making profession of faith, you become an adult member of the church and consciously affiliate with those who desire to serve God and follow Christ.

To this belongs, of course, obedience to God and Christ. The Belgic Confession states that by joining the church, we are "bowing our necks under the yoke of Jesus Christ." This yoke of Christ pertains to all that Christ has commanded. Therefore joining the church brings obligations with it. Whoever affiliates with the Christian church must also live as a Christian.

According to Article 28, bowing our necks under the yoke of Christ consists in "maintaining the unity of the church, submitting ourselves to the doctrine and discipline thereof." One thereby assumes the responsibility to promote the unity of the church. The destruction of the body of Christ by sowing discord and division is an evil matter. A torn and divided church is always a church which bleeds from many wounds.

Furthermore, submission to the yoke of Christ means submission to the doctrine and discipline of the church. The church of Christ has her doctrine. It is not true that every minister has his own doctrine. The *church* has her doctrine, namely, the doctrine of Christ. This doctrine has been summarized and codified in her confessions. It must be a person's delight to submit to this blessed doctrine.

This implies that a person will honor the offices of the church as having been instituted by Christ, and that he believes that it pleases the Lord to instruct and govern us by them. Obviously, there will be deficiencies in both the office-bearers and their official labors. However, this never absolves us from our duty to honor them for their work's sake.

At times, there is so little respect for the offices of the church. One might respond: "The office-bearers themselves are to be blamed for this." This, however, does not absolve you from your duty. Christ has vested them with these offices and has said, "He that despiseth you despiseth me; and he that despiseth me despiseth him that sent me" (Luke 10:16).

By voluntarily affiliating with the church, we submit ourselves to Christian discipline and the admonition of the office-bearers. Do not misinterpret this submission to discipline. Both admonition and the exercise of discipline regarding life and doctrine are intended for our well-being. The Scriptures say concerning office-bearers that "they watch for your souls, as they that must give account" (Heb. 13:17).

This submission to the official ministry of the church also means that we will faithfully attend the preaching of the Word. Our Heidelberg Catechism posits that, especially on the Lord's Day, we must frequent the house of God "to hear His word, to use the sacraments, publicly to call upon the Lord, and contribute to the relief of the poor, as becomes a Christian" (Lord's Day 38).

To the place where the congregation assembles herself, God has attached this promise: "For where two or three are gathered together in my name, there am I in the midst of them and I will bless them" (Matt. 18:20). Thus, if you desire to meet the Lord, you must, together with the congregation of the Lord, place yourself under the preaching of the Word.

What a blessed message is to be heard there—a message of acquittal for guilty ones; a message of salvation for whoever believes in Christ; a message of help and comfort for whoever flees to God; and a message of eternal salvation for all who love the Lord Jesus in sincerity!

Never will the ears of men hear a more glorious message than the one that is heard in the church! There you will hear that God so loved the world that He gave His only begotten Son, so that whosoever believes in Him should not perish, but have eternal life. Who would not desire to be there?

As soon as a person is converted, he will begin to love God's house and its institutions. Then he will exclaim with David, "LORD, I have loved the habitation of thy house, and the place where thine honour dwelleth" (Ps. 26:8). He will no longer be satisfied with attending church just once on the Sabbath. There will then be a hunger and yearning for the Bread of Life.

Empty places in church are an indictment against those persons who should be sitting there. We are admonished by the apostle not to forsake "the assembling of ourselves together, as the manner of some is" (Heb. 10:25). Thus we must faithfully come to church, for Jesus, as was the custom, also went to the synagogue on the Sabbath.

No one will ever grow beyond the need to go to church. We are in need of continual instruction. Faith continually needs to be strengthened and nourished. The godly in Scripture were all very fond of assembling themselves with the congregation. They could say, "I was glad when they said unto me, Let us go into the house of the LORD" (Ps. 122:1).

Then there is the communion of saints. One believes, sings, and confesses not as an individual, but in communion with all God's children.

Sunday must therefore be a special day for us. It is the day upon which we enter the house of God to hear God's message and unitedly seek His face in prayer. We come there to listen to God's voice which speaks to us by way of His servants—and there we speak to God by way of prayer, the singing of the psalms, confession of guilt, and profession of faith.

It is of crucial importance for the Christian church to keep the Lord's Day holy. Working on Sunday, worldly pleasures, and engagement in sports threaten the observance of this blessed day. In His goodness, the Lord has given us this day. In the midst of the rush and restlessness of life, the Lord gives us a day in which we may rest from our labors so that we devote ourselves entirely to the things of God's kingdom. Bowing our neck under the yoke of Christ also means that we will keep the Lord's Day holy.

Article 28 of the Belgic Confession concludes by saying, "...and as mutual members of the same body, serving to the edification of the brethren, according to the talents God has given them." Thus, if the Lord has given us gifts, we are to use them for the well-being of His church. Not every one has received the same gifts from God. There is also a need for "hewers of wood and drawers of water" (Josh. 9:21). It is therefore rather sad that when something needs to be done in the church, it is nearly always done by the same people.

Behold, this is the yoke of Christ! An unrenewed person will say, "What an unbearable yoke! Who can bear this?" The regenerate, however, do understand what is expressed in Matthew 11:29-30, "Take my yoke upon you, and learn of me; for I am meek and lowly in heart: and ye shall find rest unto your souls. For my yoke is easy, and my burden is light."

When you love God and Christ, the yoke of Christ will be so easy and His burden so light! When reflecting upon this, Samuel Rutherford said, "Lord Jesus, thy rebukes are sweeter to me than the kisses of the world."

In this manner, a person, upon Christ's command, joins himself to the church and bows his neck under His blessed yoke. For he who calls God his Father, calls the church his mother.

— 11 —
PROFESSION OF FAITH AND THE WORLD

The Consequences of Making Profession of Faith
Upon having made public profession of faith before God and His church, a person has now enlisted in the service of King Jesus. He has professed publicly whom he desires to serve. As a consequence of this profession, he therefore has the sacred calling to "let your conversation be as it becometh the gospel of Christ" (Phil. 1:27). Nobility obligates!

The Lord Jesus taught, "Whosoever therefore shall confess me before men, him will I confess also before my Father which is in heaven. But whosoever shall deny me before men, him will I also deny before my Father which is in heaven" (Matt. 10:32-33).

We are therefore duty-bound to confess Him whom we have confessed within the walls of the church wherever God has placed us—at work, within the circle of our friends, and upon encountering all whom the Lord causes to cross the pathway of our life.

Anyone who has a baptized forehead and has made public profession of faith cannot live as the world lives. The Lord calls you to live a radically different life.

How many there are who think after having made profession of faith, "That's behind us." This is not true, however. It is but the beginning, for all who have made profession of faith now have a sacred calling—the calling to be different from the world. The Lord had been very gracious to the people of Israel. By His mighty hand He had led them out of Egypt. The apostle states in 1 Corinthians 10 that they all passed through the Red Sea and that they were all baptized unto Moses in the cloud and in the sea. What a magnificent reality this was!

And yet, with many of them, God was not well pleased. Why not? Because they lusted after evil things. The apostle then quotes Exodus 32:6 as being applicable to most of the Israelites: "The people sat down to eat and drink, and rose up to play" (1 Cor. 10:7). They committed fornication and murmured, for the spirit of the Egyptian world still dwelt in their hearts. Even though they had been led out of Egypt, Egypt still remained in the heart of many.

We also live in such a world. We live during a period and among people who eat, drink, fornicate, and murmur. May we who have made profession of faith participate in this? May we dwell in their company? No, we may not. We have been baptized! We bear the distinguishing mark of King Jesus. We have made profession of faith and sworn allegiance to His banner. We are therefore now called to do what our baptism requires: "forsake the world, crucify our old nature, and walk in a new and holy life."

In the World and not of the World

Many people from other nations deem it a privilege to be able to live in either North America or Western Europe. In these parts of the world, there is prosperity, freedom of speech, and a good social support system—an ideal world in which to live.

However, for a Christian it is a very dangerous world! We are surrounded by what the world has to offer—namely, "the lust of the flesh, and the lust of the eyes, and the pride of life" (1 John 2:16). The Western world has degenerated from a Christian society to a pagan society. It is a process that is still in motion. Our culture wants to eradicate whatever reminds her of Christian morality and Christian tradition. The remains of a Christian civilization must be eliminated. In its place comes a humanistic world-life-view in which man himself is the norm for what he does and desires. Our Western society is becoming a godless society in which few have any regard for God and His Word.

This can be noticed in a variety of ways. Whoever goes to church on Sunday will be the exception and will often be the only one to do so in the street in which he resides. One will be mocked when he lets it be known in the work place that he believes in God and the Bible and desires to live according to God's laws. At best, there will be some respect for his views, but then as a worldlife view which no longer belongs to our age. And even if he is tolerated, he will no longer be understood.

We are called to live and work in this world, and our Christianity must become visible in this world. This is, however, nothing new. The position of a Christian has never been any different. The world has always been hostile toward God. This was true both before and after the flood, and it was true before and after the birth of Christ.

The Scriptures speak of the world in very negative terms, especially in the letters of John. There is a sharp antithesis between true believers and the world. The world is the domain of evil and is in bondage to Satan. Satan is called the prince of this world. Believers, on the contrary, are not of this world and have come out from among her.

The world in which we live lies in wickedness. Ever since the fall in Paradise, Satan has taken the reins of this world, and goes about as a roaring lion and an angel of light, seeking whom he may devour.

However, this world is at the same time the place where Christ gathers His church. It is here, in this evil world, that He has His church, gathered unto Himself and chosen unto eternal life.

If you could have a bird's-eye view of the spiritual disposition of this world, everything would appear black and defiled. You would have to say with Paul, "There is none that understandeth, there is none that seeketh after God" (Rom. 3:11).

However, upon closer examination, you would discover that there are nevertheless some white spots upon this spiritual map of the world. Those are the places where Christ has built His church and Satan's power has been broken. These white spots reveal the coming of God's kingdom.

Nevertheless, there are but few white spots in our dark world, and upon those places where the light of the gospel has been, it becomes at times dark again. The world continues to lie in wickedness. Such will be the situation until the return of Christ.

The kingdom of Jesus is not of this world, and God's children are therefore strangers and pilgrims in this world. By grace, they are citizens of the kingdom of heaven and no longer of this world. They look for that "city which hath foundations, whose builder and maker is God" (Heb. 11:10).

The life of the Christian is therefore referred to as a pilgrimage.

The more our society gravitates away from biblical norms and values and the less traces of Christian morality are to be found, the more this will become a reality for all who love the Lord Jesus in sincerity. Our present situation will increasingly resemble the situation in which the early Christians found themselves.

The early Christians truly lived in a godless world. The moral decadence of the first centuries was great. It was a world which resembles our present world. This, among other things, becomes evident in the film based on the book *Satyricon*, written by Petronius who was a contemporary of Nero. It is noteworthy that the modern man of our Western culture found this film appealing. People recognized and were prepared to accept the morality that came to the foreground in this film.

The lead character of this book is Encolpius. He is a fornicator, homosexual, liar, and thief. Yet, he maintains that his way of life is normal. He claims that he has a right to indulge in pleasure and to be what he wants to be. The story begins in a brothel. It then proceeds to give an account of a journey through southern Italy, interspersed with numerous sexual escapades, and concludes with a description of one of the most lewd orgies of antiquity. Again, it is noteworthy that Western man endorses this lead character and approves of his morality.

Juvenalis (60-140 A.D.) also describes the decadence of the Roman culture. It is he who coined the phrase "bread and games." He writes: "How greatly the majesty of the Romans has declined! Formerly they dominated the world and governed all affairs. Now there are but two things toward which all their wishes and desires are inclined: 'bread and games.'"

Roman culture had become a decadent culture which had but few traces of its former greatness and lofty ethics. And how did Christians live in this world?

The Example of the Early Christians
Probably the clearest description of how Christians viewed their position in this world is given by Diognetes (175 A.D.):
> Christians do not differ from others by the places in which they live, nor by the language they use or the morals they espouse.

Nowhere do they live in their own cities, nor do they speak a unique language, nor is their manner of existence extraordinary. Their doctrine is neither the invention of the ingenuity of busily occupied humanity, nor are they, as others, proponents of human notions.

However, though they live in both Greek and non-Greek cities, dependent upon their circumstances, and adhere to the traditions of the land in regard to dress, food, and other matters pertaining to daily life, nevertheless they manifest a lifestyle which is generally recognized as both unique and strange.

They live in their own country—but as strangers. They share in all things as fellow citizens, and yet in all things must endure being treated as strangers. Each foreign country is their homeland and each country is foreign to them.

They marry just as anyone else would. They have children, but do not abandon them. They share their tables but not their beds. They live "in the flesh," but not "according to the flesh."

They reside upon the earth, but are at home in heaven. They obey the laws of the land, but in their own lives they exceed the norms of these laws. They love everyone, and yet are persecuted by all. They are unknown, and yet they are murdered. They die, and yet they are made alive.

They are poor, but they make many rich. They are lacking in everything, and yet they have everything in abundance. They are dishonored, and yet this constitutes their glory. They are slandered, and yet they are justified. They are reviled, and yet they bless. They are insulted, and yet they honor others. When they perform acts of benevolence, they are punished as evildoers.

When they are punished, they rejoice as if they are stimulated by this. They are treated by the Jews as outcasts, and the Greeks persecute them. And those who hate them, cannot give any reason for their hostility.

Thus, the Christians occupied their place in the world, but were at the same time not of the world. They were, so to speak, citizens of two worlds. In the world, they faithfully engaged in their occupation, but at the same time they were citizens of the kingdom of heaven. They fulfilled their obligations as citizens, but at the same time their conversation was in heaven from where they expected their Lord.

They occupied every position in society in which they were not compelled to act contrary to God's Word, and refused to be involved in anything that was contrary to God's Word. The apostles had taught them to conduct themselves thus in the world. In church, they heard the following preaching:

> Dearly beloved, I beseech you as strangers and pilgrims, abstain from fleshly lusts, which war against the soul; having your conversation honest among the Gentiles: that, whereas they speak against you as evildoers, they may by your good works, which they shall behold, glorify God in the day of visitation. Submit yourselves to every ordinance of man for the Lord's sake: whether it be to the king, as supreme; or unto governors, as unto them that are sent by him for the punishment of evildoers, and for the praise of them that do well. For so is the will of God, that with well doing ye may put to silence the ignorance of foolish men: as free, and not using your liberty for a cloak of maliciousness, but as the servants of God. Honour all men. Love the brotherhood. Fear God. Honour the king (1 Pet. 2:11-17).

Christians were not called to escape the world. Rather, they were called to manifest their faith in God and live in harmony with His commandments in a pagan culture.

They were also called to live as strangers. Peter uses here the word *paroika*, from which our words "parochial" and "parish" are derived. The Christian church was a community of strangers whose home was elsewhere. The congregations were parishes—that is, communities of strangers. Their loyalty was to God and not to the world.

However, being a stranger manifested itself in the midst of a profane world—in the very first place, by their way of life. The Christians did not participate in the sinful excesses of the heathens. They lived a new life. They lived according to the commands and precepts of Christ, their Lord and Savior.

The early Christians drew attention *by their lives*. And indeed, it was as such that the pagans assessed Christianity as an entirely new and entirely different way of life. Justin Martyr writes of this:

> Previously we found delight in uncleanness—now in cleanness. Previously we engaged in black magic—now we are devoted to the good and eternal God. Previously money and possessions

were supremely valued by us—now we share with each other what we possess and give to whoever is in need. Previously we hated and murdered one another and refused to eat with people of a different race—however, now that Christ has appeared, we have fellowship with one another, pray for our enemies, and seek to win over to our side all who hate us without a cause.

Then there was also fraternal fellowship. The early church was truly a community. There was mutual care for each other. Within the church community, care was extended to widows and orphans, slaves sat next to their masters, the sick were cared for, and prisoners were visited.

Praamsma writes correctly that "in a world in which egotism and lust for pleasure were dominant, this living sermon (a sermon of deeds) made a deep impression."

The Example of the Early Christian Martyrs

The early church was a martyr church, consisting of people who were prepared to die for their faith. The majority of executions took place in a circus-like atmosphere, as entertainment for the masses.

To this belonged the beastly (in the literal sense of the word!) spectacle of the martyrs' struggle with wild animals. Naked and sometimes wounded due to the torture they were subjected to, Christians were driven into the arena. In unison the people would cry out, "Death to the ungodly!" Or they would cry out, "*Salvum lotum, salvum lotum*," that is, "I wish you a delightful bath." Thus they would mock with the blood-covered martyrs.

Such mocking, however, would not last very long. For instance, when in the stadium of Carthage the blood-covered martyr Saturus was repeatedly assaulted by wild animals and the people were screaming, "Salvum lotum, salvum lotum," their mocking changed into fear and dread. Saturus willingly endured the torture inflicted upon him and his face began to shine. He began to speak of the fact that Christ was with Him and he cried out, "Resurrection, resurrection!"

This faith of the Christians in the world to come and in the judgment before God's judgment seat made the world very uncomfortable. For this reason they not only burned the remains of the executed Christians, but their ashes were dispersed in the river in order to attempt to destroy their hope in the resurrection. In Carthage, they even removed the bones of Christians from their graves in order to burn them and scatter their ashes to the wind. The pagans did everything in their power to crush this faith in life eternal. It must not, should not, and would not be true that there would be a judgment and eternal life after death!

Such were the life and death of the early Christians. They were not of this world. However, their being strangers in this world did not make them recluses. Though strangers, they were turned toward the world. Their Christianity had a message for and manifested compassion toward the world.

The early Christians believed resolutely that Jesus was the only hope for the world—the only way to be reconciled with God. Apart from faith in Jesus, man could only expect eternal death.

This faith was one of the great incentives for mission work during the first centuries of Christianity. The early Christians truly believed that without Christ people would be eternally lost.

Justinus says it very plainly: "Hell is a place where all shall be punished who have lived an ungodly life and did not believe that those things would come to pass which God has taught us through Christ." That understanding caused them to speak with compassion to their fellowmen. This touching compassion for their fellowmen and their deep joy about what they themselves had found in Christ made a deep impression on many.

Citizens of two Worlds

The early Christians were citizens of two worlds—not in the sense of being a Christian on Sunday and a citizen of the world during the week, but while they sojourned on earth, their conversation was in heaven and their heart was with God and Christ. As long as they were not yet in heaven, God and Christ were with them. The words of Jesus, "Lo, I am with you alway, even unto the end of the world" (Matt. 28:20), were very real to them. For the early Christians, there was an intimate relationship between their daily lives and their being a Christian. And yet, their home was not here below. They knew themselves to be strangers and pilgrims who looked for a better country.

This is how we ought to live after having professed the name of God and Christ publicly. On the one hand, the Christian is a citizen of the nation in which he resides, but on the other hand the true Christian is a citizen of the kingdom of heaven. His conversation is upon earth, and yet his conversation is in heaven.

How can we be like this and still live in this world? This is only possible when one has become a new creature as a result of regeneration and has been united to Christ by a true faith. Without regeneration, we ultimately still belong to this world—and without knowledge of the love of Christ, love for the world will be the dominating force of our lives.

Attempts to live a holy life before God apart from faith in Christ will only lead to a cold and legalistic self-righteousness. Only they who as lost sinners have become acquainted with the love of God in Christ will have a desire to walk uprightly before God. We need this in the very first place. Only then will we be able to serve God and confess Christ in this world.

Only when the Holy Spirit unites us with Christ who is in heaven will there be a seeking of the things which are above where Christ Jesus is at the right hand of the Father. Then we will not seek those things which are on earth (Col. 3:1-2).

By nature we are (as is true of all men) of the earth, earthy. When Calvin deals with the subject of meditating upon the future life, he begins by saying, "How strongly we are inclined by nature to a slavish love of this world" (*Institutes,* 3.9.1).

How we all are entangled in covetousness, lust for pleasure, and all manner of sin! The affections of fallen man have become so blunted that his life often does not transcend the life of the beast. Animals are satisfied when they can eat and mate. Frequently, people have no higher desires than that.

In light of this, how true are the words of Jesus: "Marvel not that I said unto thee, Ye must be born again" (John 3:7)! God must again become the highest purpose of our lives. It is God who has given us life. He alone has a just claim upon our hearts. How obligated we are to return everything to Him!

When God converts a person, a longing after God will be born in his heart. His heart will cry out after Him more than a hart pants after the waterbrooks. To miss God is the most difficult thing that can happen to him. How he will then grieve over sin, for it is sin that makes separation between God and his heart! The Lord will then again become the supreme object of his affection. He will then see so much worthiness in God that he will say, "Even if there were neither hell nor heaven, yet do I desire to serve and fear Thee."

He will then understand Augustine who said, "O God, we are created unto Thee, and our heart will remain restless until it finds rest in Thee."

This constitutes the beginning of being a stranger upon earth. Then there will be times that he longs to be forever with the Lord so that he will never again have to sin.

In true conversion, a person will become acquainted with the Lord Jesus. Not only will he perceive how greatly he has sinned against the Lord, but it will also become a grievous reality that he is continually inclined toward all evil. The way of self-improvement becomes a dead-end road. He will be compelled to say, "With me things are only becoming worse. My heart is polluted and evil. From my side it is a hopeless case!" However, it is in that way that Jesus Christ becomes precious for such a person. His ears will then be open for the message of the gospel in which Jesus exclaims, "Come unto me, all ye that labour and are heavy laden, and I will give you rest" (Matt. 11:28).

When, as a lost and ungodly sinner, you may look upon Jesus—that is, how He has endured the punishment and borne the curse in the stead of hell-worthy sinners, and you may find peace in the blood of His cross—a longing will then be kindled in your heart to live for Him and to follow Him through thick and thin. How this will motivate a person to be a stranger in this world!

In true conversion, the Lord will teach us self-denial and our flesh will be crucified. This bestial love for the world will then be crucified in us. The Lord will frequently use the cross and adversity to accomplish this. Our view of the cross and adversity is so wrong. Paul says, "Whom the Lord loveth he chasteneth, and scourgeth every son whom he receiveth" (Heb. 12:6).

Cross-bearing and trials will teach us that our home is not here below and will see to it that we do not feel at home here below.

Their purpose is to make us strangers here below. It will teach us that this life is full of sorrow, trouble, and misery, and that we do not have an abiding city here below.

The well-known Thomas Boston said that whenever he wanted to lay down in the nest of this world, the Lord would put a sharp thorn in that nest.

How blessed are we when we may say that the cross has decreased our love for this world! Then we will no longer see this world as being rich and full, but as poor and empty. We will then join Asaph in saying, "It is good for me to draw near to God" (Psa. 73:28).

Everything ultimately boils down to two options: Either you will be conquered by the world or you will conquer the world. Calvin said, "There is no medium between the two things: the earth must either be worthless in our estimation, or keep us enslaved by an intemperate love of it" (*Institutes*, 3.9.2).

When heaven becomes our home, the earth will be nothing more than a place of exile. When it becomes our chief delight to enjoy the presence of God, we will no longer be able to find our chief joy in this world.

This does not mean, however, that we may not enjoy the good things which the Lord grants us. Marriage, the family, friends, a vocation, youth, nature, and so many other things are also God's gifts. We may be grateful for them. They are God's gifts bestowed upon us to serve Him and to thank Him for them. All these things also come from the Lord. Calvin wrote, "Therefore, while this life serves to acquaint us with the goodness of God, shall we disdain it as if it did not contain one particle of good?" (*Institutes*, 3.9.3).

We may not become so attached to this world's goods that they become our chief joy. We are called to be strangers in this world, and yet not be strange to this world! Christians are not hermits who withdraw themselves entirely from this world. We do not walk around with blinders. Rather, we need to be conscious of what goes on in the world. We are not monks who attempt to keep the world outside of the walls of the monastery.

A Christian stands with both feet in the midst of this world and knows that God has given him a task there. Nevertheless, he has caught sight of a better country.

This life must be for us a place in which we are as strangers. The Christian is a pilgrim who is journeying to that city which has foundations, whose builder and maker is God. His heart will yearn for this. This will be his comfort in the midst of affliction. One day he will ever be with the Lord. It will cause him to say, "Oh bliss which cannot be measured! O joy which banishes all sorrow! There our pilgrimage will be forgotten; and there we will be at home!"

Witnesses

The Lord Jesus prayed, "I pray not that thou shouldest take them out of the world" (John 17:15). Jesus did not ask His Father to remove true believers out of this world. They must remain in the world, for the Christian has a calling here. Jesus said to His disciples, "Ye are the salt of the earth," and "Ye are the light of the world" (Matt. 5:13-14).

He also said to them, "Thou shalt be my witnesses" (Acts 1:8). However, not only were the apostles called to bear witness to Jesus, but all Christians are called to do so. They are called to confess Christ before men. Bearing witness and confessing are, therefore, intimately connected with one another. The church may not be silent in the world. It is the will of Jesus that true believers would be His witnesses in the world.

The verb "to witness" is the equivalent of the Greek word "martureo." Our word "martyr" has been derived from it, for in the ancient world bearing witness to the truth that Jesus is the Son of God would frequently go hand in hand with martyrdom.

The Christian witness consists of this: that Jesus is truly the Son of God. This testimony is never a take-or-leave-it proposition. Precisely because it is only Jesus Christ, the Son of God, who saves from death and the curse, this testimony will always be accompanied by the call to repentance and faith. He who is a witness for Christ will call sinners to break with a sinful world, and his objective will be to lead them to faith in Christ. In such a testimony, it will be unmistakably declared that he who neither repents of his sins nor believes in Christ shall perish forever. It is exactly this latter aspect which prompted the world to oppose the testimony of the Christians and frequently resulted in the witness becoming a martyr. Christians truly believed that whoever did not believe in Christ would perish forever.

Tertullian therefore pleaded with the people to repent and flee the wrath to come: "Do not ignore the future. We who have no fear ourselves, are not trying to make you fearful. Rather, we wish that we could rescue all men by warning them not to resist God. Therefore, since we grieve over your ignorance, pity you for your human error, and consider your future, the threatening signs of which are evident every day, we are compelled to speak to you in this manner."

From the accounts of martyrs, one gets the impression that the issue is not so much whether the martyr remained steadfast, but how the judges responded to their testimony.

It is known of the martyr Hermes of Adrianapolis that he so earnestly warned his judges about their impending eternal perdition while calling them to faith in Christ that the presiding judge, Justinus, exclaimed, "You speak as if you are capable of changing me into a Christian." So the pagans were called to come to grips with the message.

The early Christians were witnesses. Slaves spoke to their masters, merchants testified in the marketplace, and the common women spoke in the bath houses. They could not remain silent about what they had found in Christ. That is what made the early church so effective in her outreach. During the early centuries of Christianity, there was hardly any organized mission effort, and yet the church grew very rapidly. Every Christian was a missionary. They could not remain silent about the hope which was in them.

Profession of faith must be followed by bearing witness. Evangelism must not only be conducted by way of organized evangelistic outreach. The best approach will always be to use encounters with those who belong to our circle of family and friends, or those with whom we work or attend school.

Our testimony must proceed from a personal faith. When we personally believe that all who remain outside of Christ shall perish forever, we will be compelled to bear witness. And if we have personally become acquainted with the saving power of the blood of Jesus, we will be compelled to speak to others about Christ. Knowing the power of the gospel will lead to its proclamation.

How can we recommend the Bread of Life if we have not eaten from it ourselves? We will not be able to be silent about the One whom we love and to whom we owe our salvation. We will then desire to bear witness to what He means to us. Thus it will be with the person who, conscious of the need and guilt of his life, has become acquainted with Jesus. Sooner would the stones speak than that such persons could be silent!

This is something entirely different than what is so often heard in certain circles: "I wish to testify about my faith." Such compulsive witnessing does more harm than good. Such a person often merely wishes to prove that he is a Christian. If we had to bear witness to our faith, we would soon be finished. No, we must bear witness of Christ and of what God in Christ is willing to be for a sinner.

On the other hand, however, we may not remain silent about the hope which is in us. Our modern world says, "Religion is a private matter. One must not bother others with it. It is something for Sunday and for private use."

True witnesses will, however, not be able to be silent. We read of the apostles that they were forbidden by the Sanhedrin to speak about Jesus. But the apostles responded by the mouth of Peter, "We cannot but speak the things which we have seen and heard" (Acts 4:20).

We must, however, not only witness with words, but especially with our lives. Our lives must be a living witness. The world can ignore your words, but not your life. Therefore, we must especially bear witness with our lives. We do not have to preach to prove that we are Christians. The best sermon is a godly life.

The early Christians drew attention by their different way of life. They were different from the world. In their marriages and families, they displayed purity and care for one another. Moral purity and faithfulness were highly esteemed by the early Christian church.

The old world was characterized by sexual promiscuity and egotism. One did not care for the elderly, invalids, and chronically ill in their society. The Christians, on the contrary, drew attention by their hospitality, mutual love, and the care they extended to the sick, the elderly, the handicapped, and prisoners. The world noticed their love, their joy because of the salvation they had found in Christ, their new way of life, their purity, their self-sacrificial spirit, and their genuine care for their fellowmen. It drew attention and aroused curiosity. During a time which was as pleasure-oriented, materialistic, and promiscuous as our own, the world saw in Christianity a manner of life, and, above all, a manner of dying, which was to be observed nowhere else.

It is this which we again need in our age. Then the world will be prepared to listen to the Christian church.

In a proper manner, we must be "different" from the world. When an innocent and honest man is locked up with a group of rowdy prisoners, the prisoners will notice that this man is different and that he really does not belong with them.

Our lifestyle is, therefore, of such importance. It will often mean that one will not be able to participate. Frequently, one will have to say "no," and, consequently, be mocked for it. Know, however, that you are then in good company. "Wherein they think it strange that ye run not with them to the same excess of riot, speaking evil of you" (1 Pet. 4:4).

Lifestyle
In Romans 12:2, the apostle says, "And be not conformed to this world, but be ye transformed by the renewing of your mind." This text pertains to our heart. In the first place, we are not to be conformed to this world inwardly.

That which the world deems to be of utmost value and beauty, and to be most desirable, is, for the Christian, not most valuable and desirable. For the Christian, God is the highest good and Christ is the pearl of great value.

However, the words of Paul also pertain to our exterior appearance. Also externally, we are not to be conformed to the world.

What temptations there are in the world—especially in the world of today! Many things which God condemns in His Word are commonplace in the world. I only need to refer to the sexual immorality which prevails. By working and living in this world, we are confronted with views which oppose a life in the fear of God.

It is in the midst of this world that Paul exclaims, "Be not conformed to this world." That is the calling of all who have made profession of faith. By doing so, we have chosen God and His service.

We must, therefore, demonstrate to the world to whom we belong and whom we serve. We will then be unable to do what the world does or endorse the world's agenda.

This must proceed, however, from the renewing of your mind. Renewal is necessary. Your heart and mind must be different from that of the world—yes, your very principles must be different. Without an inward renewal of the heart, we will espouse the same principles as the world.

Paul warns as strongly against the appearance of godliness, which denies its power, as he does against world conformity. A person can outwardly be pious and live a very strict life. However, if this does not proceed from love to God, one will be no more than a whitened sepulcher. Everything will be no more than an empty shell.

If, however, a person has learned to love God and his heart cries out after God, his life cannot but be different. Yes, when one may be acquainted with Christ and God's forgiving love, his position in this world will be different. Our external walk will then be changed from the inside out.

Many say, "The outside does not matter." Indeed, external customs are no guarantee that there is genuine godliness. Nevertheless, the fear of God does manifest itself in our lifestyle—and thus also on the outside.

Scripture gives us directions regarding this. Our apparel must be modest and honorable (cf. 1 Tim. 2:9; 1 Pet. 3:3-4). Clothing has been provided to cover our nakedness. The difference between male and female must be evident in clothing and hairstyle. It is, for example, shameful for a woman to have her head shorn (1 Cor. 11:6).

God says that it is an abomination to Him when a man wears a woman's garment and when a woman dresses herself as a man (Deut. 22:5). Of course, I hear someone say, "It is not in the clothes." Nevertheless, our external appearance is a mirror of our heart. There is a connection between our inner life and our external appearance. There is clothing which a Christian young man or a Christian young woman will refuse to wear. Calvin says concerning this:

> The manner in which one is dressed is in and of itself not a matter of such great weight. However, since it is a shame when men are feminized, it is equally shameful when a woman seeks to as-

sert herself by way of male garments and conduct. Therefore a modest and honorable walk is prescribed here. The best preservation of modesty is therefore a modest form of dress (*Commentary* on Deut. 22:5).

Perhaps you may say, "What then is permitted? How shall I dress myself?" There is an old adage which says, "One must be dressed in such a fashion that the world will not laugh at you and that God's people will not weep over you." Our dress must be modest and honorable.

Scripture likewise speaks about all manner of make-up and seductive clothing. Hear how the prophet Isaiah, in his penitential message to Israel, addresses the made-up women with their wanton eyes: "Moreover the LORD saith, Because the daughters of Zion are haughty, and walk with stretched forth necks and wanton eyes, walking and mincing as they go, and making a tinkling with their feet" (Isa. 3:16).

Also the use of television is an expression of world-conformity. By having a TV, one truly brings the world into his home. Together with the books and music of the world, it completes the picture. One has then become like the world. The antithesis has then vanished.

Therefore, let it be evident in your lifestyle that you wish to serve the Lord. Do not ask, "How far may I go?," but rather, "Lord, what wilt Thou have me to do?"

— 12 —
PROFESSION OF FAITH AND THE GOOD FIGHT OF FAITH

A Spiritual Soldier or a Lip-professor?
At your baptism, this petition was uttered in the prayer of thanksgiving:
> Be pleased always to govern these baptized children by Thy Holy Spirit...that then they...may acknowledge Thy fatherly goodness and mercy which Thou hast shown to them and us, and live in all righteousness under our only Teacher, King and High Priest, Jesus Christ; and manfully fight against and overcome sin, the devil and his whole dominion.

In this prayer, the congregation asks God to assist its baptized children in the spiritual battle they must wage. At baptism, a baptized child receives the royal insignia of Christ and is obligated to fight the good fight of faith under His banner. One could say that a military oath has been sworn. Therefore, as the child reaches maturity, he will be called upon to engage in holy warfare.

To engage in this battle, one must turn to Christ in His three offices as Prophet, Priest, and King. Only then can the battle be fought in a rightful and godly manner, and will victory be attained.

When you make profession of faith, this battle awaits you. You have sworn to be loyal to the banner of King Jesus. Not only has this been seen and witnessed in the midst of Christ's church, but it is also known in the camp of the enemy. Satan knows that you have sworn allegiance to the banner of King Jesus. He will not readily accept this, but will attempt to make you unfaithful and lead you to apostasy. The apostle therefore urges, "Fight the good fight of faith, lay hold on eternal life, whereunto thou art also called, and hast professed a good profession before many witnesses" (1 Tim. 6:12).

A Christian is a soldier. Jesus also taught this, for He said, "Strive to enter in at the strait gate" (Luke 13:24).

Many people faithfully attend church on Sunday, say their prayers, read their Bibles, and keep God's commandments, and their names are recorded in the membership register of the church. They all hope that upon death they shall enter heaven.

However, they are not acquainted with spiritual warfare—with an internal conflict between the flesh and the spirit and an external battle with the world. They have no knowledge of crucifixion of the flesh, of self-denial, and of being ridiculed and maligned by the world, let alone of being harassed and assaulted by the evil one. And yet, they believe that they are Christians and that soon they shall become partakers of eternal bliss. This is neither the Christianity described for us in the New Testament nor that which was preached by Jesus and the apostles.

Three Arch-enemies

The true Christian is a soldier and must do battle with a three-headed enemy: the world, the devil, and his own sinful flesh. These are the three mortal enemies of the true Christian, and therefore one must wage war against them after having made profession of faith.

The world will become your enemy. Now that you are desirous to serve God and Christ, you will notice that the world is dangerous territory for the Christian. How full the world is of snares and pitfalls!

The pleasures of the world will draw you away from God and Christ. The mockery of the world will hinder you in taking a stand for God and Christ. You will always be in danger of participating with the world, being one with the world. However, James says, "Whosoever therefore will be a friend of the world is the enemy of God" (James 4:4).

The devil will become your enemy. Satan is the old enemy—an enmity that dates back to Paradise. Since the fall of Adam and Eve, he goes about as a roaring lion and an angel of light, seeking whom he may devour.

He knows that you have sworn allegiance to the banner of Jesus and that you are ready to desert his army, or that, by grace, you have already done so and no longer do his bidding. It will now be true of you what Jesus said to Peter, "Simon, Simon, behold, Satan hath desired to have you, that he may sift you as wheat" (Luke 22:31).

Satan is frequently the invisible enemy who wears a mask. He can act piously. Luther called Satan "the white devil." By making all sorts of pious or wicked suggestions and insinuations in your evil heart, he will try to draw you away from God and His service. He will attempt to render Christ and the gospel suspect by undermining your hope in God's grace.

The worst enemy is your own flesh. Even after conversion, your fallen nature will be inclined toward evil. The old man has indeed been dethroned, but has not died. Time and again, the old nature will seek to reclaim its former territory. Sin will even cleave to you in your most holy activities.

What warfare this engenders in the heart of a regenerated person! The apostle Paul could say that with the inner man he delighted in the law of God. But at the same time he had to say, "But I see another law in my members, warring against the law of my mind, and bringing me into captivity to the law of sin which is in my members" (Rom. 7:23).

How distressing the power of indwelling sin and the wickedness of our hearts can be! The great apostle cried out, "O wretched man that I am! who shall deliver me from the body of this death?" (Rom. 7:24). Therefore, you cannot do battle against these enemies in your own strength, but only "under our only Teacher, King and High Priest, Jesus Christ."

If you had the nature of an unfallen angel and were not a fallen creature, you would be able to wage this war in your own strength. However, having to deal with a corrupt heart, a tireless devil, and an enticing world, you must learn with the godly Jehoshaphat, "We have no might against this great company that cometh against us." Then you may also join him in saying, "But our eyes are upon thee" (2 Chr. 20:12).

What a great grace it is to look unto Jesus Christ, our Prophet, so that in your blindness you may learn where you must seek your strength! What a gracious blessing it is that Jesus is the King who is stronger than all your enemies, and that He is the High Priest who prays for you at God's right hand and who has compassion with all your weaknesses! Only by looking to Him will you be able to wage this battle.

The Christian soldier is therefore not a person who relies upon his own strength and weaponry. Instead, he prays the prayer recorded in our Heidelberg Catechism:

> Since we are so weak in ourselves, that we cannot stand a moment; and besides this, since our mortal enemies, the devil, the world, and our own flesh, cease not to assault us, do Thou therefore preserve and strengthen us by the power of Thy Holy Spirit, that we may not be overcome in this spiritual warfare, but constantly and strenuously may resist our foes till at last we obtain a complete victory (Q & A 127).

Engagement in this warfare is a good sign. It proves that you no longer find delight in sin and that Satan is no longer your master.

Dead fish float along with the stream, whereas living fish swim against the stream. The worst chains are the ones that are not felt. As a result of conversion, the chains of bondage begin to oppress and this Egyptian bondage will cause one to cry out to God.

The warfare will also flare up when, out of the love in your heart, you are desirous to serve the Lord. Spiritual warfare will commence when the choice is born in one's heart, "As for me and my house, we will serve the Lord" (Josh. 24:15).

Jesus taught, "When a strong man armed keepeth his palace, his goods are in peace: but when a stronger than he shall come upon him, and overcome him, he taketh from him all his armour wherein he trusted, and divideth his spoils" (Luke 11:21-22). Jesus is saying here that as long as you serve the devil willingly, there will be no spiritual warfare. However, when one becomes the recipient of the grace of conversion, and you bid Satan and the world farewell in order to serve God, the devil will launch his assault.

After Israel had left Egypt, Pharaoh pursued them with horses and wagons in order to bring them into captivity again. When the choice has been born in one's heart and one has bid farewell to all evil, he will experience that the devil will be his enemy. Precisely when you desire to serve the Lord, he will oppress you and attempt to recapture you.

How discouraging it can be when you experience that so much

of the world still remains in your heart! How frequently, and in spite of our presumed capability to do otherwise, we fall into sin and must learn, "For I know that in me (that is, in my flesh,) dwelleth no good thing" (Rom. 7:18)!

Yet, such experiences are necessary. One must learn not to expect anything from his own strength. Acquaintance with your own heart and the experience of your own weakness will teach you to wage this battle by faith.

When looking upon ourselves—that is, when we consider how weak we are and how powerful sin is, how devious Satan is and how enticing the world is—we would despair. However, in the hour of need, faith looks to Christ and says, "My eyes are upon Thee!" It looks to Christ, the Advocate in heaven, and to His blood and righteousness. Then, in spite of all warfare, one may say, "Nay, in all these things we are more than conquerors through him that loved us" (Rom. 8:37).

In spite of all that transpires in this warfare, it is a good fight. We are waging war under the leadership of the best King. He is acquainted with this warfare. He knows your enemies and your weaknesses, and He has promised: "Be of good cheer! I have overcome the world."

Furthermore, the battle which God's children must wage is a battle which has already been won. Christ has already gained the victory and, therefore, you will eventually triumph eternally in Him. The promise, "He that overcometh, the same shall be clothed in white raiment; and I will not blot out his name out of the book of life" (Rev. 3:5), is not made to "fair weather" and nominal Christians, but to spiritual warriors.

Falling into Sin Through Weakness

In the *Form for the Administration of Baptism* we read,

> And if we sometimes through weakness fall into sin, we must not therefore despair of God's mercy, nor continue in sin, since baptism is a seal and undoubted testimony that we have an eternal covenant of grace with God.

The Bible gives us examples of falling into sin through weakness. Noah, Abraham, David, Peter, and others exemplify the weakness of the greatest of the saints. James says, "For in many things we offend all" (James 3:2). When God's children fall into sin, Satan will attempt to make them despair of God's grace. That is always his evil objective. First he will tempt us to sin, and then he will torment us by insinuating that there is no forgiveness for such sins.

In the midst of a fall into sin, however, one must not despair of God's mercy. Baptism declares to us that we have to do with a God who is faithful and with whom there is much forgiveness. Calvin therefore states: "Wherefore, as often as we fall, we must recall the remembrance of our baptism, and thus fortify our minds, so as to feel certain and secure of the remission of sins" (*Institutes*, 4.15.3). The Christian will need the comfort of his baptism during his entire life.

The catechumens who made public profession of faith in the early church would wear a white garment for eight days. It is difficult not to soil a white garment during a period of eight days; it is equally difficult to remain unspotted in the midst of the world. God's children frequently detect that they have defiled their garments. Even if they do not fall into public sin, they frequently bend their knees at night as defiled sinners. What a comfort it then is to be reminded of the message of baptism: that as surely as water removes the filth of the body, so the blood of Jesus Christ, God's Son, cleanses from all sin! Divine forgiveness will then comfort their grieving heart and rekindle in them the zeal to persevere in sanctification and the battle against sin.

The ungodly *live* in sin, whereas the godly *fall* into sin, after which they arise again. Swine fall into the mud and feel comfortable in it, whereas a clean animal will make every effort to get out of the mud as quickly as possible.

Believers, due to weakness, fall into sin. This could also happen to you after having made profession of faith. What often becomes of our good intentions! How our hearts can prove to be as wicked as it was prior to making profession of faith! How discouraging that we do not serve the Lord as He is worthy to be served!

This does not always mean that we fall into open sin. However, our heart and thoughts can greatly defile the white garment of our confession. At such times, Satan will attempt to remove from your heart the doctrine of God's unmerited pardon and the witness of the blood of Christ which speaks better things than the blood of Abel. He will then cry to you, "For such a person as you there is no salvation with God. If your profession of faith had been genuine, you would be living a more holy and godly life. If there were any trace of the grace of regeneration in you, you would not have such a struggle with sin and you would live a holy life before God."

In the midst of such warfare, one must think of his baptism. For Christians in the early church, baptism signified a radical departure from sin and the world. The old life was laid aside in order that, from that moment forward, they might embrace the church of God, whose doctrine they now believed, as their new home and mother.

Though such Christians had fled from the world, the world followed them. Paul already wrote concerning this: "I wrote unto you in an epistle not to company with fornicators: yet not altogether with the fornicators of this world, or with the covetous, or extortioners, or with idolaters; for then must ye needs go out of the world" (1 Cor. 5:9-10).

The early Christians experienced the reality of this. They could not remove themselves from the world, for in that world they had to live, work, and reside. Consequently, they did at times, out of weakness, fall into sin.

Sin in the Christian and a Second Repentance

Above the life of the early Christians towered the words, "But as he which hath called you is holy, so be ye holy in all manner of conversation" (1 Pet. 1:15). By way of baptism and profession of faith, they rescinded their allegiance to the devil and the world. The bond with paganism was fully severed. The Christian formerly was a citizen of this world, but now he had become a citizen of God's kingdom and a member of the household of God. Justinus wrote:

> Formerly we found delight in immorality; now we only embrace morality. Formerly we engaged in occult practices; now we have turned to God who alone is good and without beginning. Formerly we loved money and material possessions above everything else; now we use our possessions for the common good and to give to every needy person. Formerly hatred and envy

were common among us; now we pray for our enemies and try to lead those who unjustly hate us to repentance.

This is the practical application of the Sermon on the Mount.

The early Christians spoke to heathens about the renewal of their lives. Cyprian of Carthage testifies:

When I still lived in the darkness of the night and was tossed to and fro upon the uncertain waves of my life and roamed about in a world of vacillating fortune, I could not accept the fact that someone could be born again. I could not accept that through the redeeming washing of regeneration one could lay aside what one used to be formerly—yes, that, invigorated by a new life, one's heart and affections could be changed, though one would continue his earthly existence as he did formerly.

Nevertheless, this high standard was not always maintained. Tertullian mentions that also among Christians there was pride, materialism, unholy passion, cowardice, and gambling, the vice of paganism.

The very best of Christians had to concur with Paul, "Not as though I had already attained" (Phil. 3:12). Clement confesses: "Even I am still a sinner to the core of my being and have in no wise escaped temptation." Tertullian made the well-known confession, "Since I am defiled by every imaginable sin, I was born for no other reason except to repent."

One detects in the writings of the early church fathers that they wrestled with their sins and failures subsequent to their baptism and profession of faith. They asked themselves the question, "Has all that is old truly passed away? Am I not still a heathen at heart though with my head I am a Christian? How shall I deliver myself from the thousands of snares with which the world surrounds me?"

As a reaction to these questions, there was a practice in the early church known as a second repentance. There was no other way to have peace with God except by renewed repentance and being washed in the blood of Christ. Calvin was not the first to say that one must remember his baptism. It was a message of comfort for the early Christian who, after his baptism, still found so much of sin and the world within himself. In many writings of the early church fathers you will find the expression, "Your baptism remains efficacious throughout your entire life." And indeed, the blood of Jesus always remains fresh and invigorating.

Repentance was a very important component of the teaching of the early church. A Christian needed to live a penitent life. Calvin, in spite of its abuse by Rome, adopted this view. He rejected Roman Catholic penance; however, he praised a life of penitence. It is in that way that God's image is restored in us: "In one word, then, by repentance I understand regeneration, the only aim of which is to form in us anew the image of God, which was sullied, and all but effaced by the transgression of Adam" (*Institutes*, 3.3.9).

Therefore, Calvin deems that person to have advanced the most who has learned to loathe himself the most. In this way, God's children are exercised not only in becoming better acquainted with their weakness, but also to become better acquainted with God's faithfulness, His readiness to pardon, and Christ's blood as well as to become the more earnest in pursuing sanctification.

If anyone were to think that it shall become better in the future, Calvin dismantles this vain dream. He writes: "God...cleanses them from pollution, and consecrates them as his temples, restoring all their inclinations to real purity, so that during their whole lives they may practice repentance, and know that death is the only termination to this warfare" (*Institutes*, 3.3.9).

The way to heaven is different than we anticipate at the beginning of conversion. At that time, we think and hope that we will grow in godliness, that we will become stronger in the battle against sin, that we will be delivered from doubt, and that finally we will enter heaven as truly holy and godly people.

The way, however, is so very different! The way to heaven is a way of becoming weaker in ourselves, seeing increasingly more sin in ourselves, and having no other hope but in the finished mediatorial work of Christ. Such a person will concur with Luther by saying, "Oh, my soul, you should indeed tremble were it not for the fact that King Jesus is there."

This is a good and proper way, for in this way Christ becomes increasingly precious and indispensable. This way God alone will receive the honor of our salvation.

Therefore, you ought not to be too discouraged when the way is so different than you had anticipated when making profession of faith. When you run aground with all your good intentions, and you discover more and more sin in your heart, you must bring all this to Jesus. When you stumble, you must be mindful of your baptism, which declares "that I am as certainly washed by His blood and Spirit from all the pollution of my soul, that is, from all my sins, as I am washed externally with water."

When you do not increase in either holiness or godliness, you must consider that Scripture says, "He must increase and I must decrease" (John 3:30). The Lord will leave an afflicted and poor people, of whom we read, however, that "they shall trust in the name of the LORD" (Zeph. 3:12).

There will be a struggle until the very last breath. However, it will be a good fight, for it is a battle which we will wage "under our only Teacher, King, and High Priest, Jesus Christ." When you look upon Him, you will be comforted and strengthened in the way. Salvation is secure in His sacrifice and intercession. However weak you may be in yourself, you will be more than conquerors in Him.

Even though you will be disappointed in yourself every day, and even though you will never progress beyond "For I know that in me (that is, in my flesh,) dwelleth no good thing: for to will is present with me; but how to perform that which is good I find not" (Rom. 7:18), it is nevertheless a good fight in which the Lord will put more gladness in our hearts than in the time that the corn and the wine of the ungodly are increased (Psa. 4:7).

How blessed is then the prospect of the believer! Hear what Paul says: "I have fought a good fight, I have finished my course, I have kept the faith: henceforth there is laid up for me a crown of righteousness, which the Lord, the righteous judge, shall give me at that day: and not to me only, but unto all them also that love his appearing" (2 Tim. 4:7-8).

The way of the good fight is the way that leads to victory. Then what was already expressed at your baptism will come true for you: "We shall finally be presented without spot or wrinkle among the assembly of the elect in life eternal."